The Unfamiliar *Touch*

Lessons from the woman with the issue of blood

BISHOP DR. JOSEPH C. KANU

The Unfamiliar Touch
(Lessons from the woman with the issue of Blood)

© 2022 Bishop (Dr.) Joseph C. Kanu

All right reserved: No part of this publication may be reproduced, retrieved or stored in any retrieval system; electronically, mechanical or otherwise without the written permission of the author and the publisher.

Unless otherwise indicated, all scripture quotations are taken from the King James Version of the Bible.

ISBN: 978-1-100-21769-7

Book cover design and Printing by tmacre8tv@gmail.com (+2348137371249)

Formatted by Framedwordsintl (+2348139410461)

The Unfamiliar Touch
(Lessons from the woman with the issue of Blood)

Table of Content

- Acknowledgment 9
- Dedication 10
- Foreword 11
- Chapter One 13
- Touch 13
- Introduction 13
- Its significance 14
  - Touch as Defilement 15
  - Touch as Anointing 17
  - Touch as Strengthening and Encouragement 24
  - Touch for Healing and Grace 27
  - Touch as Sanctification 30
  - Touch As Ministry and Service 32
  - Touch As Evidence 34
  - Touch As Discernment 35

The Unfamiliar Touch
(Lessons from the woman with the issue of Blood)

The issue of blood (Mark 5:25-35), (Luke 8: 43-44) and (Matthew 9:20-22) 36

"Who touched me?" 40

Chapter Two..44

Her Issue of Blood – Diagnosis....................44

Introduction..44

Twelve years: The Meaning..............................45

Uncleanliness 47

Psychic trauma 49

The Doctor's reports 50

- Doctor Of Theology 52
- Doctor Of Psychology 53
- Doctor Of Chemistry...............................53
- Traditional Doctors 54
- The Herbalist Doctor...............................54
- The Spiritualist or Witch Doctor.............55

Deterioration 55

Chapter Three..60

Jesus 60

Introduction..60

The Unfamiliar Touch
(Lessons from the woman with the issue of Blood)

She heard about him..61

His renown (Mark 1: 21-28) 64

Healings and deliverance (Mark 1: 40-45).......68

Spreading the word 70

Chapter Four..87

The other side 87

Introduction..87

The power of Prayer...87

Barriers to Breakthroughs 90

- Identifying the barrier 91
- Seeking God's direction 92
- Listening to God 93
- Keeping your focus on Jesus, not the barrier..93
- Rehearsing God's victories 94
- Staying in faith..94
- Rebuke 96
- We are for signs and wonders 99

Chapter Five...105

Nothing to Lose 105

The Unfamiliar Touch
(Lessons from the woman with the issue of Blood)

Introduction 105
- Actively taking part in church services .. 110
- Practicing forgiveness 111
- Charity 111
- Reading inspirational books 111
- Conversing with God daily 112
- Power of Faith 112

Chapter Six 117

Divine Idea I – Disguise 117

Introduction 117

Its significance 118

Its reward 122

Chapter Seven 125

Divine Idea II – His Garment 125

Introduction 125

Its meaning 125

Its significance 127

Identity 129
- Authority: 129
- Dignity: 130

The Unfamiliar Touch
(Lessons from the woman with the issue of Blood)

- Status and Prosperity: 130
- The unfamiliar touch 130
- Ways to touch Jesus 133
  - Giving your life to him 134
  - Becoming a soul winner 135
  - His Word 135
- Our Faith 136
  - Our Works 137
  - Giving 138

Chapter Eight 140

The woman with the issue of blood – Lessons 140

- Introduction 140
- She heard the word of God. 141
- Ideas 142
- She put faith into action 143
- Decision 144
- She knelt down - Position of Prayer 146
- She prostrated - Position of Worship - Warships for Welfare 147
- She crawled - Position of Perseverance - Overcoming offense 149

The Unfamiliar Touch
(Lessons from the woman with the issue of Blood)

Disappointment to This Appointment 153
Introduction 153
Its meaning 153
Do not despair 154
Chapter Ten 161
Seeking attention 161
Introduction 161
Its meaning 161
Its significance 162
Why we need it 163
Its reward 164
His Will be done 165
Prayer points 171
Altar call to receive Christ 178
About the Author 181
Contact Details 186

The Unfamiliar Touch
(Lessons from the woman with the issue of Blood)

Acknowledgment

I wrote this book by the inspiration of the Holy Spirit and I want to thank God for granting me the grace to write.

I want to use this opportunity to thank God for His grace that removes disgrace, His fame that removes shame and for how far He has brought me in a short while.

The Unfamiliar Touch
(Lessons from the woman with the issue of Blood)

Dedication

I want to dedicate this book to The Holy Spirt because He is my source. To my parents, siblings, family, children, mother in love, especially my wife who works behind the scenes for the success of our family and ministry. To my spiritual father, church family, spiritual sons and daughters. I love you all.

**The Unfamiliar Touch
(Lessons from the woman with the issue of Blood)**

Foreword

In 2015, God gave me this message. I personally wrote it down in a book as a sermon. Whenever this message was preached, people responded to God in an unprecedented way.

Also, I realized that like the woman with the issue of blood, several people have issues affecting them in live. Sometimes, these issues take over the person's identity. The woman had a name but due to her issue of blood, she was referred to as a woman with the issue of blood.

This book isn't only about the woman with the issue of blood but how anyone with issues could touch Jesus with an unfamiliar touch for an uncommon miracle.

In the story of the woman with the issue of blood, everyone presumably

The Unfamiliar Touch
(Lessons from the woman with the issue of Blood)

touched Jesus with a familiar touch but her touch was unfamiliar. It drew healing virtue from Jesus for her healing.

God will do the same for you as you reach out in faith.

The Unfamiliar Touch
(Lessons from the woman with the issue of Blood)

Chapter One
Touch

Introduction

In this chapter, we shall discuss the meaning of touch, its spiritual significance in our lives and the various types of touch. Furthermore, we shall briefly discuss the biblical story of the woman with the issue of blood in this chapter and in subsequent ones.

Its meaning

To touch means to bring a bodily part into contact with another or an object, in order to perceive through the tactile sense. It also means to handle or feel

The Unfamiliar Touch
(Lessons from the woman with the issue of Blood)

gently usually with the intent to understand or appreciate. However, the spiritual sense of touch is a symbol for our closeness to the Divine, the feeling of being embraced and of belonging.

The sense of touch is far more intimate than smell. It is as though our hearts have caught the scent, and then we move closer in order to be immersed in it—to be enveloped, to be touched. The presence of God is not only an irresistible attraction, but through touch, we are unified in our inmost being—we experience oneness.

Its significance

Spiritually, a Divine touch can be defined as a heavenly touch, a transforming and power-giving touch that empowers an ordinary man to do

**The Unfamiliar Touch
(Lessons from the woman with the issue of Blood)**

the extraordinary. It is a touch that gives a new identity to the touched. It is a touch that is different from the ordinary touch of a friend, a colleague or even a spouse.

Furthermore, touch has a very important and far-reaching place in each of our lives. There are many different angles that we can look at it from – all of which can teach us something of the spiritual realm.

- **Touch as Defilement**

Under the Old Covenant, there were many laws given about touching unclean things that would bring defilement. One side of this is highlighted in Leviticus 5:2-3 KJV:
(2) Or if a soul touch any unclean thing, whether it be a carcase of an

The Unfamiliar Touch
(Lessons from the woman with the issue of Blood)

unclean beast, or a carcase of unclean cattle, or the carcase of unclean creeping things, and if it be hidden from him; he also shall be unclean, and guilty.
(3) Or if he touch the uncleanness of man, whatsoever uncleanness it be that a man shall be defiled withal, and it be hid from him; when he knoweth of it, then he shall be guilty.

On the other side, we also have the fact that when someone who was "unclean" touched something, then that object too would become defiled. Numbers 19:22 KJV says: *"And whatsoever the unclean person toucheth shall be unclean; and the soul that toucheth it shall be unclean until even."*

The Unfamiliar Touch
(Lessons from the woman with the issue of Blood)

- **Touch as Anointing**

In his message entitled *'Transmitting God's Power'* which deals with the laying on of hands, Derek Prince says the following: "The function of laying on of hands in commissioning people is used to recognise but not appoint, the persons of God's choice. It is used to set apart a person to a certain task or ministry. It is used to endorse a person with authority. And it is used to equip a person with all the spiritual authority or gifts that person will need."

We have numerous examples of this in both the Old and New Testament. In the Old Testament, we recall the stories when Jacob (Israel) blesses Joseph's sons (Genesis 48) and when

The Unfamiliar Touch
(Lessons from the woman with the issue of Blood)

Moses anoints Joshua (Numbers 27:18-20 and Deuteronomy 34:9).

Genesis 48:1-22 (1) And it came to pass after these things, that one told Joseph, Behold, thy father is sick: and he took with him his two sons, Manasseh and Ephraim.
(2) And one told Jacob, and said, Behold, thy son Joseph cometh unto thee: and Israel strengthened himself, and sat upon the bed.
(3) And Jacob said unto Joseph, God Almighty appeared unto me at Luz in the land of Canaan, and blessed me,
(4) And said unto me, Behold, I will make thee fruitful, and multiply thee, and I will make of thee a multitude of people; and will give this land to thy seed after thee for an everlasting possession.

The Unfamiliar Touch
(Lessons from the woman with the issue of Blood)

(5) And now thy two sons, Ephraim and Manasseh, which were born unto thee in the land of Egypt before I came unto thee into Egypt, are mine; as Reuben and Simeon, they shall be mine.

(6) And thy issue, which thou begettest after them, shall be thine, and shall be called after the name of their brethren in their inheritance.

(7) And as for me, when I came from Padan, Rachel died by me in the land of Canaan in the way, when yet there was but a little way to come unto Ephrath: and I buried her there in the way of Ephrath; the same is Bethlehem.

(8) And Israel beheld Joseph's sons, and said, Who are these?

(9) And Joseph said unto his father, They are my sons, whom God hath

The Unfamiliar Touch
(Lessons from the woman with the issue of Blood)

given me in this place. And he said, Bring them, I pray thee, unto me, and I will bless them.

(10) Now the eyes of Israel were dim for age, so that he could not see. And he brought them near unto him; and he kissed them, and embraced them.

(11) And Israel said unto Joseph, I had not thought to see thy face: and, lo, God hath shewed me also thy seed.

(12) And Joseph brought them out from between his knees, and he bowed himself with his face to the earth.

(13) And Joseph took them both, Ephraim in his right hand toward Israel's left hand, and Manasseh in his left hand toward Israel's right hand, and brought them near unto him.

(14) And Israel stretched out his right hand, and laid it upon Ephraim's

The Unfamiliar Touch
(Lessons from the woman with the issue of Blood)

head, who was the younger, and his left hand upon Manasseh's head, guiding his hands wittingly; for Manasseh was the firstborn.

(15) And he blessed Joseph, and said, God, before whom my fathers Abraham and Isaac did walk, the God which fed me all my life long unto this day,

(16) The Angel which redeemed me from all evil, bless the lads; and let my name be named on them, and the name of my fathers Abraham and Isaac; and let them grow into a multitude in the midst of the earth.

(17) And when Joseph saw that his father laid his right hand upon the head of Ephraim, it displeased him: and he held up his father's hand, to remove it from Ephraim's head unto Manasseh's head.

The Unfamiliar Touch
(Lessons from the woman with the issue of Blood)

(18) And Joseph said unto his father, Not so, my father: for this is the firstborn; put thy right hand upon his head.

(19) And his father refused, and said, I know it, my son, I know it: he also shall become a people, and he also shall be great: but truly his younger brother shall be greater than he, and his seed shall become a multitude of nations.

(20) And he blessed them that day, saying, In thee shall Israel bless, saying, God make thee as Ephraim and as Manasseh: and he set Ephraim before Manasseh.

(21) And Israel said unto Joseph, Behold, I die: but God shall be with you, and bring you again unto the land of your fathers.

The Unfamiliar Touch
(Lessons from the woman with the issue of Blood)

(22) Moreover I have given to thee one portion above thy brethren, which I took out of the hand of the Amorite with my sword and with my bow.

Numbers 27:18-20 (18) And the LORD said unto Moses, Take thee Joshua the son of Nun, a man in whom is the spirit, and lay thine hand upon him;
(19) And set him before Eleazar the priest, and before all the congregation; and give him a charge in their sight.
(20) And thou shalt put some of thine honour upon him, that all the congregation of the children of Israel may be obedient.
Deuteronomy 34:9 And Joshua the son of Nun was full of the spirit of wisdom; for Moses had laid his hands

The Unfamiliar Touch
(Lessons from the woman with the issue of Blood)

upon him: and the children of Israel hearkened unto him, and did as the LORD commanded Moses.

The New Testament also provides a record regarding this, for Paul said to Timothy: *"Do not neglect the gift that is in you, which was given to you by prophecy with the laying on of hands of the eldership." 1 Timothy 4:14*

- **Touch as Strengthening and Encouragement**

There are numerous passages where the Lord or His host of angels touched His servants to give them strength and encouragement. Below are certain examples:

The Unfamiliar Touch
(Lessons from the woman with the issue of Blood)

Daniel in particular, experienced this sort of touch more than once for: *"Now, as he was speaking with me, I was in a deep sleep with my face to the ground; but he touched me, and stood me upright."* (Daniel 8:18) and then again in chapter 10, *"Suddenly, a hand touched me, which made me tremble on my knees and on the palms of my hands."* (10) ..."*And suddenly, one having the likeness of the sons of men touched my lips; then I opened my mouth and spoke, saying to him who stood before me, My lord, because of the vision my sorrows have overwhelmed me, and I have retained no strength." v16* ... *"Then again, the one having the likeness of a man touched me and strengthened me."*

The Unfamiliar Touch
(Lessons from the woman with the issue of Blood)

Also in Jeremiah 1:8-9, we read *"Do not be afraid of their faces, for I am with you to deliver you,* says the Lord." Then the Lord put forth His hand and touched my mouth, and the Lord said to me: *"Behold, I have put My words in your mouth."*

Furthermore, John experienced this sort of strengthening again in Revelation 1:17 where it reads: "And when I saw Him, I fell at His feet as dead. But He laid His right hand on me, saying to me, *do not be afraid; for I am the First and the Last."* Although we may not all experience these "open" visions of heavenly beings, we all need the Lord's touch nonetheless to strengthen and encourage us.

The Unfamiliar Touch
(Lessons from the woman with the issue of Blood)

- **Touch for Healing and Grace**

Famously considered as one of the most popular aspects of touch, the accounts of touch for Healing and Grace in the Bible are too numerous to list. However, even in our modern time, touch is still used for healing and to impart grace. Jesus goes before us where He touches the infirm and even the dead and brings wholeness and life. Sometimes we think of a healing touch as putting a hand on a head or shoulder and praying, but Jesus shows us a different way – He put His fingers in ears, spat and touched a mute tongue, reached out in compassion and touched the leper, spat on blind eyes and Mark tells us

The Unfamiliar Touch
(Lessons from the woman with the issue of Blood)

that *"And as many as touched Him were made well."*

The other side of Touch for Healing and Grace is that because of the creative and healing power flowing from Jesus, Luke tells us that, *"the whole multitude sought to touch Him, for power went out from Him and healed them all." (Luke 6:19)*. There is also the beautiful story of the children being brought to Jesus *"that He might touch them"* because the parents recognised that His touch conveyed blessing and grace.

When we consider ourselves, what are our personal views on healing? Do we seek healing primarily from God or the doctors? It is true that Healthcare professionals offer a wonderful service to society, but we must also

The Unfamiliar Touch
(Lessons from the woman with the issue of Blood)

remember to keep our eyes on the Lord and let Him choose whether He heals us directly or through doctors.

For a better understanding of this, read the story of King Asa in 2 Chronicles 16:12 KJV: *"And Asa in the thirty and ninth year of his reign was diseased in his feet, until his disease was exceeding great: yet in his disease he sought not to the LORD, but to the physicians."*

When we do seek God, do we limit Him in the methods accept or do we cry out for mercy no matter how the Lord chooses to send it? Are we like the multitude who press in to Jesus to touch Him, or do we watch Him from afar? When we press in, let us remember that the number one reason that we should be pressing in is not

The Unfamiliar Touch
(Lessons from the woman with the issue of Blood)

just for a gift of healing or provision, but because it satisfies our deep need for relationship.

- **Touch as Sanctification**

To sanctify simply means to make holy. The author of Hebrews says that we should *"pursue… holiness, without which no one will see the Lord." (Hebrews 12:14).*

We know that under the Old Covenant, the Israelites were made holy through the sacrifices which covered their sins. In the New Covenant, Jesus, the Lamb of God was slain to wash away our sins.

In the book of Isaiah, the author relates a story where God brought conviction that he(the author) was "a

The Unfamiliar Touch
(Lessons from the woman with the issue of Blood)

man of unclean lips", but God also provided a remedy: *"Woe is me, for I am undone! Because I am a man of unclean lips, and I dwell in the midst of a people of unclean lips; for my eyes have seen the King, The Lord of hosts."*

Then one of the seraphim flew to me, having in his hand a live coal which he had taken with the tongs from the altar. And he touched my mouth with it, and said: *"Behold, this has touched your lips; your iniquity is taken away, and your sin purged." Isaiah 6:5-7*

Hebrews 9:12-14 KJV juxtaposes the two covenants beautifully: *(12) "Neither by the blood of goats and calves, but by his own blood he entered in once into the holy place,*

The Unfamiliar Touch
(Lessons from the woman with the issue of Blood)

having obtained eternal redemption for us.

(13) For if the blood of bulls and of goats, and the ashes of an heifer sprinkling the unclean, sanctifieth to the purifying of the flesh:

(14) How much more shall the blood of Christ, who through the eternal Spirit offered himself without spot to God, purge your conscience from dead works to serve the living God?"

- **Touch As Ministry and Service**

As with most good things, there is a potential that we expect them for ourselves, but unfortunately, we usually fail to give them to others. In his booklet *'Orphans, Widows, the Poor and Oppressed'*, Derek Prince

The Unfamiliar Touch
(Lessons from the woman with the issue of Blood)

says: "The key to happiness is not being loved, it is having someone to love – that's what makes life exciting!" We shouldn't just hope that others will touch us in ministry and service, but be the first to do it to others.

In many cases, loneliness can be erased from us by finding people to serve and to love. If anyone had the right to be separated and superior, it was Jesus and yet He chose to minister and serve people and as He did so, He touched them at every level. True, its not always easy to be warm with people whom you are serving if you don't ever touch them. However, if you still need healing in the area of touch, then it is better not to touch than to do so insincerely or inappropriately.

The Unfamiliar Touch
(Lessons from the woman with the issue of Blood)

Touch can be a powerful evidence which backs up what we are saying.

- **Touch As Evidence**

Following Jesus' resurrection, John relates how Jesus used touch as evidence for Thomas: And after eight days His disciples were again inside, and Thomas with them. Jesus came, the doors being shut, and stood in the midst, and said, "Peace to you!" Then He said to Thomas, "Reach your finger here, and look at My hands; and reach your hand here, and put it into My side. Do not be unbelieving, but believing." John 20:24-27

The Unfamiliar Touch
(Lessons from the woman with the issue of Blood)

Touch can be a powerful evidence which backs up what we are saying. Touch as evidence is a safety net that helps us to test our beliefs. It also helps others to test us to determine the genuineness of our faith

- **Touch As Discernment**

In 1 John 1:1, part of John's evidence for the truth that Jesus was who He claimed to be, was *"That which…our hands have handled"*.

When a doctor does an examination, obviously he doesn't just observe you and ask questions, he examines by touching so that he can discern a lump, an inflammation, a rupture, a rhythm, a fracture and so forth. Touch is a form of testing and discernment that helps us to make better informed and rational decisions.

**The Unfamiliar Touch
(Lessons from the woman with the issue of Blood)**

The issue of blood (Mark 5:25-35), (Luke 8: 43-44) and (Matthew 9:20-22)

Mark 5:25-35 KJV (25) "And a certain woman, which had an issue of blood twelve years,

(26) And had suffered many things of many physicians, and had spent all that she had, and was nothing bettered, but rather grew worse,

(27) When she had heard of Jesus, came in the press behind, and touched his garment.

(28) For she said, If I may touch but his clothes, I shall be whole.

(29) And straightway the fountain of her blood was dried up; and she felt

The Unfamiliar Touch
(Lessons from the woman with the issue of Blood)

in her body that she was healed of that plague.

(30) And Jesus, immediately knowing in himself that virtue had gone out of him, turned him about in the press, and said, Who touched my clothes?

(31) And his disciples said unto him, Thou seest the multitude thronging thee, and sayest thou, Who touched me?

(32) And he looked round about to see her that had done this thing.

(33) But the woman fearing and trembling, knowing what was done in her, came and fell down before him, and told him all the truth.

(34) And he said unto her, Daughter, thy faith hath made thee whole; go in peace, and be whole of thy plague.

The Unfamiliar Touch
(Lessons from the woman with the issue of Blood)

(35) While he yet spake, there came from the ruler of the synagogue's house certain which said, Thy daughter is dead: why troublest thou the Master any further?"

Luke 8:43-44 KJV (43) "And a woman having an issue of blood twelve years, which had spent all her living upon physicians, neither could be healed of any,

(44) Came behind him, and touched the border of his garment: and immediately her issue of blood stanched."

Matthew 9:20-22 KJV (20) "And, behold, a woman, which was diseased with an issue of blood twelve years, came behind him, and touched the hem of his garment:

The Unfamiliar Touch
(Lessons from the woman with the issue of Blood)

(21) For she said within herself, If I may but touch his garment, I shall be whole.

(22) But Jesus turned him about, and when he saw her, he said, Daughter, be of good comfort; thy faith hath made thee whole. And the woman was made whole from that hour."

In Mark 5:25-34, we see a woman named Veronica (meaning "true image"), according to the apocrypha Acts of Pilate and later tradition, which gave other details of her life, in whom the heritage of sorrow manifested as an issue of blood for twelve years. She had suffered numerous hardships from many physicians. She had spent all that she had and was no better, but rather grew worse. Imagine the feeling of

The Unfamiliar Touch
(Lessons from the woman with the issue of Blood)

hopelessness and desperation. At this point in her life, only a divine touch could put an end to her years of agony and sorrow. Then one day, she came across the Great Physician, Jesus Christ. Her faith was so strong; she believed in her heart that all she needed from Him was a passive divine touch. She believed that based on the power in the divine touch, she did not need an active touch for her to be made whole. This singular act of faith was commended by Jesus Himself.

"Who touched me?"

Jesus had realized at once that healing power had gone out from him, so he turned around in the crowd and asked, *"Who touched my clothes?"*

The Unfamiliar Touch
(Lessons from the woman with the issue of Blood)

To an extent, we know and understand why the woman had wanted to be healed secretly. Clearly part of her motivation surely had to do with the fact that, by touching Jesus, she would make him ritually unclean. This would not be something one should do to a Jewish holy man. No doubt the healed woman expected Jesus to be angry with her and the crowd to rebuke her for soiling Jesus' ceremonial status.

When the woman fell before Jesus, trembling with fear, she admitted what she had done. However, Jesus simply responded, *"Daughter, your faith has made you well. Go in peace. Your suffering is over."* Recall in that reading that there was no mention of uncleanness or even anger. Just affirmation and good news.

The Unfamiliar Touch
(Lessons from the woman with the issue of Blood)

So why did Jesus call out this woman by bringing her action into the light? Because In part, he sought to reassure her, even calling her with the intimate address, *"Daughter."*

In part, Jesus wanted to hold her up as a paragon of faith. And, in part, he wanted all to know that she was healed and restored as a full member of their community. Physical healing was the occasion for a deeper and wider restoration.

I believe that in this chapter, we have greatly grasped a broad understanding of touch, both physically and spiritually.

The Unfamiliar Touch
(Lessons from the woman with the issue of Blood)

Furthermore, we can see that in this chapter, a certain woman afflicted with a medical condition received her miracle.

The story continues in the next chapter, and may we receive our miracles like she did in the mighty name of Jesus, Amen.

The Unfamiliar Touch
(Lessons from the woman with the issue of Blood)

Chapter Two

Her issue of bLood – Diagnosis

Introduction

This is the second chapter of this spiritually enlightening book, and we shall shed more light on this woman who was afflicted with the issue of blood for twelve years as mentioned in the previous chapter. Furthermore, we shall delve deeper medically with the purpose of understanding what this condition that tormented this woman really was.

The Unfamiliar Touch
(Lessons from the woman with the issue of Blood)

Twelve years: The Meaning

Twelve years translates to 144 months.

Twelve years translates to 625.714 weeks.

Twelve years translates to 4,382.91 days

Twelve years translates to 105,120 hours

Twelve years translates to 6,307,200 minutes

Twelve years translates to 378,432,000 seconds

The figures above give numerous translations on the duration of Veronica's (based on research, her name has been identified as Veronica according to the *apocrypha Acts of Pilate and later tradition*, which gave

The Unfamiliar Touch
(Lessons from the woman with the issue of Blood)

other details of her life) issue of blood and a better understanding of how long she endured this misfortune. The woman with issue of blood had twelve years of bleeding, and pains every day for twelve years.

That is; 144 months, 625.714 weeks. 4,382.91 days, 105,120 hours, 6,307,200 minutes and 3,784,320,00 seconds of constant bleeding.

The first miracle she received wasn't that she was healed but that she was alive to witness her healing. People can die from blood loss but hers didn't kill her. What A miracle!

No matter what you are going through right, May God keep you alive until

The Unfamiliar Touch
(Lessons from the woman with the issue of Blood)

you witness your major miracle in Jesus mighty name.

Uncleanliness

According to the law (Leviticus 15:25-27):

(25) And if a woman have an issue of her blood many days out of the time of her separation, or if it run beyond the time of her separation; all the days of the issue of her uncleanness shall be as the days of her separation: she shall be unclean.

(26) Every bed whereon she lieth all the days of her issue shall be unto her as the bed of her separation: and whatsoever she sitteth upon shall be unclean, as the uncleanness of her separation.

The Unfamiliar Touch
(Lessons from the woman with the issue of Blood)

(27) And whosoever toucheth those things shall be unclean, and shall wash his clothes, and bathe himself in water, and be unclean until the even.

excessive blood flow made a woman ceremonially unclean. Any furniture she touched was unclean as well. If other people touched anything that she had touched, they would be unclean as well.

Because of the continual bleeding, the woman would have been continually regarded in Jewish law as a *'Niddah'* or menstruating woman, and so ceremonially unclean. In order to be regarded as clean, the flow of blood would need to stop for at least seven days. But because of the constant bleeding, this woman lived in a continual state of uncleanness which

The Unfamiliar Touch
(Lessons from the woman with the issue of Blood)

would have brought upon her social and religious isolation.

It would have prevented her from getting married - or, if she was already married when the bleeding started, would have prevented her from having intercourse with her husband and might have been cited by him as grounds for divorce.

Psychic trauma

In those days, women were considered unclean for being on their periods; so a woman with such a pervasive issue would literally have been ostracised by everybody within her community - including her family, assuming she had any at all (the Bible never made reference to such). It therefore not only hindered other people's relations with her (as they

The Unfamiliar Touch
(Lessons from the woman with the issue of Blood)

wouldn't have wanted to be made unclean themselves by being in contact with her), but it also restricted her ability to interact and mix with others. So this was a lady who was very much on the fringes of society. So we can deduce that this was a very troubled, stigmatized, infamous and emotionally distraught woman who had to endure this medical and emotional affliction for twelve years.

The Doctor's reports

The woman's condition, which is not clear in terms of a modern medical diagnosis, is simply translated as an "issue of blood" in the King James Version and a "flux of blood" in the Wycliffe Bible and some other versions. In scholarly language she is often referred to by the original New Testament Greek term as the

The Unfamiliar Touch
(Lessons from the woman with the issue of Blood)

Haemorrhoissa (ἡ αἱμορρooῦσα, "bleeding woman"). The text describes her as γυνὴ αἱμορροοῦσα δώδεκα ἔτη (gynē haimorroousa dōdeka etē), with *Haimorroousa* being a verb in the active voice present participle ("having had a flow [rheon], of blood [haima]"). However, some scholars and medical practitioners view it as *Menorrhagia*; and others as *Haemorrhoids*.

Furthermore, it was recorded that she visited many doctors. So put simply, a doctor is anyone who has reached the peak of their career or is qualified to treat ill patients. Eg. Dr. of psychology, Dr. of philosophy, Dr. of Medicine, Dr. of Theology, Dr of Physics, Dr. of Chemistry, Dr. of arts, etc. Personally, I refer to medical doctors as Professional handlers of

The Unfamiliar Touch
(Lessons from the woman with the issue of Blood)

Diseases (PHD). So let us assume that in her quest for healing, she visited several doctors like the ones mentioned above. In addition to this, the bible actually says that she suffered several things in the hands of many doctors as recorded in Mark 5:26

Mark 5:26 And had suffered many things of many physicians, and had spent all that she had, and was nothing bettered, but rather grew worse,

- **Doctor Of Theology**

Perhaps when she visited a doctor of theology, they reminded of her sin. She may have been judged by the likes of the pharisees who didn't see far to see what God wants to do in

The Unfamiliar Touch
(Lessons from the woman with the issue of Blood)

her. She may even have come across some sadducees who were rather sad to see her and wanted her to remain sad. They may have concluded, she was not religious enough, that's why she was suffering.

- **Doctor Of Psychology**

The psychologist after observing and studying her, may have told her that she had mental health issues, cognitive problems, emotional stress and or social anxiety. That those may be the underlying reasons why she bled.

- **Doctor Of Chemistry**

They may have said the chemicals in her body are not saturated so they are not balanced.

The Unfamiliar Touch
(Lessons from the woman with the issue of Blood)

The hormone is out of order because its being secreted in a smaller quantity or even not at all, so its not able to control the bleeding.

- **Traditional Doctors**

Presumably they may have said she needed Chinese medicine or acupuncture.

- **The Herbalist Doctor**

They may have made her perform some sacrifices, drank some herbs and concoctions. She may have been told to bath in the river for ritual cleansing.

The Unfamiliar Touch
(Lessons from the woman with the issue of Blood)

- ## The Spiritualist or Witch Doctor

The mother could be a witch, the aunty or relative may be responsible for her predicament. These are some of the endless things that could have been told her.

Deterioration

One can only imagine what this unfortunate woman must have really endured at the hands of the medical practitioners at that time in history. A touch of reality is given to her story by the knowledge that she had suffered many things of many physicians and was no better but rather *"Grew Worse."* She had tried to get well. She had gone to many

The Unfamiliar Touch
(Lessons from the woman with the issue of Blood)

doctors over the years. She spent everything she had trying to be cured. Furthermore, it was recorded that the woman with the issue of blood, presumably as we are told, was rich but later became poor. She must have sold her house, jewellery, gold, animals, wardrobe, furniture, land, etc. If she had it, she sold it.

She had spent her time, energy and resources. She may have started to borrow because she had spent all she had, so from a giver, she became a borrower. As a matter of fact, according to William Barclay's commentary, it was recorded that the Talmud gave at least eleven possible cures for her ailment, but they all failed. She wasn't getting better, only worse.

The Unfamiliar Touch
(Lessons from the woman with the issue of Blood)

Some of these Talmudic remedies included:

- Proper hydration
- Eating of vitamin C-rich foods
- Addition of more iron-rich foods to the diet
- Occasional cooking in a cast-iron pot
- Consumption of herbal supplements comprising of pomegranates, ginger and myrtle fruit
- Getting enough rest and sleep
- Occasional but rigorous exercising
- Sleeping with padded underclothes
- Having sexual Intercourse
- Birth control herbs

The Unfamiliar Touch
(Lessons from the woman with the issue of Blood)

- Eating of vitamin B-rich foods like shellfish, etc

But where men failed, Christ succeeded. Down the ages men and women which no agency could reclaim have been restored by Christ. What is not possible with men is blessedly possible with God. Her disease was outstanding, yet she was swiftly healed, for as soon as she touched the hem of His garment, "straight-way the fountain of her blood was dried up."

If a person suffers for a while from a complaint and seeks no medical advice, but in the end goes to the doctor, the doctor invariably says, "You should have come to me sooner." But it is the glory of Christ that He can heal those who come late

The Unfamiliar Touch
(Lessons from the woman with the issue of Blood)

to Him. So maybe you have spent all you have in pursuit of healing, deliverance or a solution to your situation. Fret not for God is with you. So like the woman with the issue of blood, <u>don't give up!</u>

> *No matter what you are going through right now, May God keep you alive until you witness your major miracle in Jesus mighty name.*

From this chapter, we can learn more on the medical condition of this woman along with unfortunate turn of events that befell her. However, her miracle came, and we shall discuss the worker of this miracle known as...

The Unfamiliar Touch
(Lessons from the woman with the issue of Blood)

Chapter Three

Jesus

Introduction

In this chapter, I believe that the woman with the issue of blood heard about Jesus and His miracles. This gave her the faith necessary in receiving her miracle by positioning herself for breakthrough. From chapter one to chapter five, there were several miracles, including healings and deliverances done by Jesus. And as the people began to spread the word and news of His miracles all over the place, she most definitely heard them. Now lets examine what she heard.

The Unfamiliar Touch
(Lessons from the woman with the issue of Blood)

She heard about him

Mark 5:27 KJV "<u>When she had heard of Jesus</u>, came in the press behind, and touched his garment."

We know that the story of this woman takes place within a larger story. Jesus is on his way to a synagogue leader's house to heal his dying daughter (see Mark 5:21–24) when an afflicted woman causes an interruption to His progress.

Mark 5:21-25 KJV (21) And when Jesus was passed over again by ship unto the other side, much people gathered unto him: and he was nigh unto the sea.
(22) And, behold, there cometh one of the rulers of the synagogue, Jairus by

The Unfamiliar Touch
(Lessons from the woman with the issue of Blood)

name; and when he saw him, he fell at his feet,
(23) And besought him greatly, saying, My little daughter lieth at the point of death: I pray thee, come and lay thy hands on her, that she may be healed; and she shall live.
(24) And Jesus went with him; and much people followed him, and thronged him.
(25) And a certain woman, which had an issue of blood twelve years...

We also know that Jewish Law declared her to be ceremonially unclean due to her bleeding issue (Leviticus 15:25-27).

Leviticus 15:25-27 (25)And if a woman have an issue of her blood many days out of the time of her separation, or if it run beyond the

The Unfamiliar Touch
(Lessons from the woman with the issue of Blood)

time of her separation; all the days of the issue of her uncleanness shall be as the days of her separation: she shall be unclean.

(26) Every bed whereon she lieth all the days of her issue shall be unto her as the bed of her separation: and whatsoever she sitteth upon shall be unclean, as the uncleanness of her separation.

(27) And whosoever toucheth those things shall be unclean, and shall wash his clothes, and bathe himself in water, and be unclean until the even.

This meant that she would not have been permitted to enter the temple for Jewish religious ceremonies. According to the Law, anything or anyone she touched became unclean as well. The fact that she was in the

The Unfamiliar Touch
(Lessons from the woman with the issue of Blood)

crowd pressing around Jesus meant that each person who bumped into her would have become unclean, too—including Jesus. But, after twelve years of suffering, she was obviously desperate for a miracle. *"When she <u>heard</u> about Jesus, she came up behind him in the crowd and touched his cloak, because she thought, 'If I just touch his clothes, I will be healed'" (Mark 5:27–28).*

His renown (Mark 1: 21-28)

Mark 1:21-28 KJV (21) "And they went into Capernaum; and straightway on the sabbath day he entered into the synagogue, and taught.

(22) And they were astonished at his doctrine: for he taught them as one

The Unfamiliar Touch
(Lessons from the woman with the issue of Blood)

that had authority, and not as the scribes.

(23) And there was in their synagogue a man with an unclean spirit; and he cried out,

(24) Saying, Let us alone; what have we to do with thee, thou Jesus of Nazareth? art thou come to destroy us? I know thee who thou art, the Holy One of God.

(25) And Jesus rebuked him, saying, Hold thy peace, and come out of him.

(26) And when the unclean spirit had torn him, and cried with a loud voice, he came out of him.

(27) And they were all amazed, insomuch that they questioned among

The Unfamiliar Touch
(Lessons from the woman with the issue of Blood)

themselves, saying, What thing is this? what new doctrine is this? for with authority commandeth he even the unclean spirits, and they do obey him.

(28) And immediately his fame spread abroad throughout all the region round about Galilee."

In the above passage, Jesus was not simply teaching the Scriptures, but he was also proclaiming the nearness of God's kingdom and calling people to a personal response. Jesus' message was urgent: *"The kingdom of God is near!"* Jesus' message was bold and demanding: *"Repent and believe the good news!"* And he clearly had the personal authority to deliver this message. The people were amazed at Jesus, because Jesus taught them as

The Unfamiliar Touch
(Lessons from the woman with the issue of Blood)

one who had authority, and not as their own teachers of the law.

Furthermore, Jesus' authority was revealed through his confrontation with an unclean spirit (Mark 1:23-26). We live in world where evil exists and where the forces of evil still have some measure of influence.

But we also know that God is over all and that a day will come when all evil will be defeated. When we are tempted to be overwhelmed with the opposition of the world we must remember, God is in control and in the end He will make all things right. It is also through His power that we can overcome sin.

The Unfamiliar Touch
(Lessons from the woman with the issue of Blood)

And finally, when those who heard Jesus teach and saw His power over the demon were left amazed and astonished. They recognized His authority and could not keep it to themselves. Very quickly the news of Jesus and His power spread everywhere.

Healings and deliverance (Mark 1: 40-45)

Mark 1:40-45 KJV (40)"And there came a leper to him, beseeching him, and kneeling down to him, and saying unto him, If thou wilt, thou canst make me clean.

(41) And Jesus, moved with compassion, put forth his hand, and touched him, and saith unto him, I will; be thou clean.

The Unfamiliar Touch
(Lessons from the woman with the issue of Blood)

(42) And as soon as he had spoken, immediately the leprosy departed from him, and he was cleansed.

(43) And he straitly charged him, and forthwith sent him away;

(44) And saith unto him, See thou say nothing to any man: but go thy way, shew thyself to the priest, and offer for thy cleansing those things which Moses commanded, for a testimony unto them.

(45) But he went out, and began to publish it much, and to blaze abroad the matter, insomuch that Jesus could no more openly enter into the city, but was without in desert places: and they came to him from every quarter."

This passage clearly demonstrates Jesus' powers of divine healing and

The Unfamiliar Touch
(Lessons from the woman with the issue of Blood)

deliverance along with the faith necessary for the manifestation of his divine works in our lives

Spreading the word

Mark tells us the people were so amazed at what happened that they were all talking about it, and the news about Jesus began to spread quickly. Did their amazement cause the people to believe in Jesus?

In most cases, it certainly did. After Jesus drove out the unclean spirit, "the report of Jesus went out immediately everywhere into all the region of Galilee and its surrounding area" (Verse 28). When Jesus went to the house of Simon and Andrew, "they brought to him all who were sick, and those who were possessed by demons.

The Unfamiliar Touch
(Lessons from the woman with the issue of Blood)

All the city was gathered at the door" (Verse 32-33). Clearly, then, the common people believed. Later it was revealed that Jairus, a ruler of the synagogue, also believed (Mark 5: 22-23).

Mark 5:22-25 (22) And, behold, there cometh one of the rulers of the synagogue, Jairus by name; and when he saw him, he fell at his feet,

(23) And besought him greatly, saying, My little daughter lieth at the point of death: I pray thee, come and lay thy hands on her, that she may be healed; and she shall live.

(24) And Jesus went with him; and much people followed him, and thronged him.

The Unfamiliar Touch
(Lessons from the woman with the issue of Blood)

(25) And a certain woman, which had an issue of blood twelve years,

Her faith in Jesus was built and strengthened by his great and marvelous signs and wonders which were preaching the gospel, healing the sick, casting out unclean spirits and raising the dead etc. Below is the summary of all she heard about Jesus:

- **In Mark 1:21-28, a man was delivered from unclean spirits in the Synagogue (Church)**

Mark 1:21-28 (21) And they went into Capernaum; and straightway on the sabbath day he entered into the synagogue, and taught.

(22) And they were astonished at his doctrine: for he taught them as one that had authority, and not as the scribes.

The Unfamiliar Touch
(Lessons from the woman with the issue of Blood)

(23) And there was in their synagogue a man with an unclean spirit; and he cried out,

(24) Saying, Let us alone; what have we to do with thee, thou Jesus of Nazareth? art thou come to destroy us? I know thee who thou art, the Holy One of God.

(25) And Jesus rebuked him, saying, Hold thy peace, and come out of him.

(26) And when the unclean spirit had torn him, and cried with a loud voice, he came out of him.

(27) And they were all amazed, insomuch that they questioned among themselves, saying, What thing is this? what new doctrine is this? for with authority commandeth he even the unclean spirits, and they do obey him.

The Unfamiliar Touch
(Lessons from the woman with the issue of Blood)

(28) And immediately his fame spread abroad throughout all the region round about Galilee.

- **In Mark 1: v 32-39 – He combined healing and deliverance**

Mark 1:32-39 (32)And at even, when the sun did set, they brought unto him all that were diseased, and them that were possessed with devils.
(33) And all the city was gathered together at the door.
(34) And he healed many that were sick of divers diseases, and cast out many devils; and suffered not the devils to speak, because they knew him.
(35) And in the morning, rising up a great while before day, he went out,

The Unfamiliar Touch
(Lessons from the woman with the issue of Blood)

and departed into a solitary place, and there prayed.

(36) And Simon and they that were with him followed after him.

(37) And when they had found him, they said unto him, All men seek for thee.

(38) And he said unto them, Let us go into the next towns, that I may preach there also: for therefore came I forth.

(39) And he preached in their synagogues throughout all Galilee, and cast out devils.

**The Unfamiliar Touch
(Lessons from the woman with the issue of Blood)**

- **In Mark 1: v 40-45 – A leaper came to Jesus and said, if you will, you can make me clean:**

Mark 1:40-45 (40)And there came a leper to him, beseeching him, and kneeling down to him, and saying unto him, If thou wilt, thou canst make me clean.
(41) And Jesus, moved with compassion, put forth his hand, and touched him, and saith unto him, I will; be thou clean.
(42) And as soon as he had spoken, immediately the leprosy departed from him, and he was cleansed.
(43) And he straitly charged him, and forthwith sent him away;
(44) And saith unto him, See thou say nothing to any man: but go thy way,

The Unfamiliar Touch
(Lessons from the woman with the issue of Blood)

shew thyself to the priest, and offer for thy cleansing those things which Moses commanded, for a testimony unto them.

(45) But he went out, and began to publish it much, and to blaze abroad the matter, insomuch that Jesus could no more openly enter into the city, but was without in desert places: and they came to him from every quarte

- **In Mark 2: v 1-12, Jesus heals a paralytic:** Mark 2:1-12

(1) And again he entered into Capernaum, after some days; and it was noised that he was in the house.
(2) And straightway many were gathered together, insomuch that there was no room to receive them, no, not so much as about the door:

The Unfamiliar Touch
(Lessons from the woman with the issue of Blood)

and he preached the word unto them.
(3) And they come unto him, bringing one sick of the palsy, which was borne of four.
(4) And when they could not come nigh unto him for the press, they uncovered the roof where he was: and when they had broken it up, they let down the bed wherein the sick of the palsy lay.
(5) When Jesus saw their faith, he said unto the sick of the palsy, Son, thy sins be forgiven thee.
(6) But there were certain of the scribes sitting there, and reasoning in their hearts,
(7) Why doth this man thus speak blasphemies? who can forgive sins but God only?
(8) And immediately when Jesus perceived in his spirit that they so

**The Unfamiliar Touch
(Lessons from the woman with the issue of Blood)**

reasoned within themselves, he said unto them, Why reason ye these things in your hearts?
(9) Whether is it easier to say to the sick of the palsy, Thy sins be forgiven thee; or to say, Arise, and take up thy bed, and walk?
(10) But that ye may know that the Son of man hath power on earth to forgive sins, (he saith to the sick of the palsy,)
(11) I say unto thee, Arise, and take up thy bed, and go thy way into thine house.
(12) And immediately he arose, took up the bed, and went forth before them all; insomuch that they were all amazed, and glorified God, saying, We never saw it on this fashion.

**The Unfamiliar Touch
(Lessons from the woman with the issue of Blood)**

- **In Mark 4: v 35-41 – Jesus calmed the storm**

Mark 4:35-41 (35)And the same day, when the even was come, he saith unto them, Let us pass over unto the other side.

(36) And when they had sent away the multitude, they took him even as he was in the ship. And there were also with him other little ships.

(37) And there arose a great storm of wind, and the waves beat into the ship, so that it was now full.

(38) And he was in the hinder part of the ship, asleep on a pillow: and they awake him, and say unto him, Master, carest thou not that we perish?

(39) And he arose, and rebuked the wind, and said unto the sea, Peace, be

The Unfamiliar Touch
(Lessons from the woman with the issue of Blood)

still. And the wind ceased, and there was a great calm.
(40) And he said unto them, Why are ye so fearful? how is it that ye have no faith?
(41) And they feared exceedingly, and said one to another, What manner of man is this, that even the wind and the sea obey him?

- **In Mark 5: 1-20 Jesus cast legion into swine:**

Mark 5:1-20 (1)And they came over unto the other side of the sea, into the country of the Gadarenes.
(2) And when he was come out of the ship, immediately there met him out of the tombs a man with an unclean spirit,

The Unfamiliar Touch
(Lessons from the woman with the issue of Blood)

(3) Who had his dwelling among the tombs; and no man could bind him, no, not with chains:

(4) Because that he had been often bound with fetters and chains, and the chains had been plucked asunder by him, and the fetters broken in pieces: neither could any man tame him.

(5) And always, night and day, he was in the mountains, and in the tombs, crying, and cutting himself with stones.

(6) But when he saw Jesus afar off, he ran and worshipped him,

(7) And cried with a loud voice, and said, What have I to do with thee, Jesus, thou Son of the most high God? I adjure thee by God, that thou torment me not.

(8) For he said unto him, Come out of the man, thou unclean spirit.

The Unfamiliar Touch
(Lessons from the woman with the issue of Blood)

(9) And he asked him, What is thy name? And he answered, saying, My name is Legion: for we are many.

(10) And he besought him much that he would not send them away out of the country.

(11) Now there was there nigh unto the mountains a great herd of swine feeding.

(12) And all the devils besought him, saying, Send us into the swine, that we may enter into them.

(13) And forthwith Jesus gave them leave. And the unclean spirits went out, and entered into the swine: and the herd ran violently down a steep place into the sea, (they were about two thousand;) and were choked in the sea.

(14) And they that fed the swine fled, and told it in the city, and in the

The Unfamiliar Touch
(Lessons from the woman with the issue of Blood)

country. And they went out to see what it was that was done.

(15) And they come to Jesus, and see him that was possessed with the devil, and had the legion, sitting, and clothed, and in his right mind: and they were afraid.

(16) And they that saw it told them how it befell to him that was possessed with the devil, and also concerning the swine.

(17) And they began to pray him to depart out of their coasts.

(18) And when he was come into the ship, he that had been possessed with the devil prayed him that he might be with him.

(19) Howbeit Jesus suffered him not, but saith unto him, Go home to thy friends, and tell them how great

The Unfamiliar Touch
(Lessons from the woman with the issue of Blood)

things the Lord hath done for thee, and hath had compassion on thee.
(20) And he departed, and began to publish in Decapolis how great things Jesus had done for him: and all men did marvel.

- ## In Mark 5: v21-24 Jesus was on his way to Jairus's house

Mark 5:21-24 (21)And when Jesus was passed over again by ship unto the other side, much people gathered unto him: and he was nigh unto the sea.
(22) And, behold, there cometh one of the rulers of the synagogue, Jairus by name; and when he saw him, he fell at his feet,
(23) And besought him greatly, saying, My little daughter lieth at the

The Unfamiliar Touch
(Lessons from the woman with the issue of Blood)

point of death: I pray thee, come and lay thy hands on her, that she may be healed; and she shall live.
(24) And Jesus went with him; and much people followed him, and thronged him.

From what we can conclude from this chapter, it's without a doubt that she heard many wonderful and marvelous works performed by Jesus.

Furthermore, we shall discuss certain acts we must perform or endure in the next chapter to unlock our breakthroughs and miracles. I pray that our breakthroughs shall locate us this hour in the mighty name of Jesus. Amen.

The Unfamiliar Touch
(Lessons from the woman with the issue of Blood)

Chapter Four

The other side

Introduction

In this Chapter, we shall emphasize the power of prayer and shed more light on rebuke. We shall also look into the barriers of breakthrough and our God given potentials.

The power of Prayer

Proverbs 18:21 "Death and life are in the power of the tongue: and they that love it shall eat the fruit thereof."

Prayer is a form of communication with God. Simply put, prayer is talking to God. Prayer is a weapon that *"has divine power to demolish strongholds. We demolish arguments and every pretension that sets itself up*

The Unfamiliar Touch
(Lessons from the woman with the issue of Blood)

against the knowledge of God, and we take captive every thought to make it obedient to Christ."- 2 Corinthians 10: 4-5. The Bible urges us, *"And pray in the Spirit on all occasions with all kinds of prayers and requests. With this in mind, be alert and always keep on praying for all the saints" (Ephesians 6:18).*

And the prayer of faith will save the one who is sick, and the Lord will raise him up. And if he has committed sins, he will be forgiven. Therefore, confess your sins to one another and pray for one another, that you may be healed. The prayer of a righteous person has great power as it is working.

The woman with the issue of blood was led by the Holy Spirit to position

The Unfamiliar Touch
(Lessons from the woman with the issue of Blood)

herself for healing. Guided by the Holy Spirit and fueled by prayer, she moved quietly, inspirationally, and passionately.

Her following the leading of the God who carried her in the direction of Jesus exemplifies her faith; yet, no verbal that she is a believer in Jesus was said.

Her body as a single voice of prayer, protested against sickness, and as an evangelistic model of justification dragged herself gracefully into the crowd (i.e., community) in search of healing. However, the Bible does not indicate that she intentionally or rudely bumped into the other people in the crowd or that she spoke to them rudely, she simply *"came behind him, and touched the border of his garment:*

The Unfamiliar Touch
(Lessons from the woman with the issue of Blood)

and immediately her issue of blood stanched" (Luke 8:44, KJV)

God, through prayer, opens eyes, changes hearts, heals wounds, and grants wisdom (James 1:5).

The power of prayer should never be underestimated because it draws on the glory and might of the infinitely powerful God of the universe. Daniel 4:35 proclaims, "All the peoples of the earth are regarded as nothing.

> ***Prayer is a weapon that "has divine power to demolish strongholds.***

Barriers to Breakthroughs

Everyone faces barriers in life. There are many kinds of barriers – physical, emotional, spiritual, circumstantial,

The Unfamiliar Touch
(Lessons from the woman with the issue of Blood)

financial, educational, cultural, societal, and other limitations that can stop us from moving forward in life. To live life to the fullest and achieve God's best for our life, we must be able to overcome these barriers and possess the promises God has for us.

Every barrier has a solution. And there is definitely a breakthrough for you with God's help. Certainly nothing is too difficult. God's Word has the answer for life's most challenging barriers. The following are seven proven steps to overcoming any barrier you face:

- **Identifying the barrier**

If you do not know what is stopping you, then unfortunately you cannot overcome it or eliminate it. Often we

The Unfamiliar Touch
(Lessons from the woman with the issue of Blood)

are the cause of our own obstacles and we continue to keep digging a deeper hole. The first step to exiting a holes is, "If you are in one, stop digging". To exercise our faith, we need to know what mountain to speak to.

- Seeking God's direction

Breaking through barriers in life does not come easily or naturally to any of us. Neither does submitting to the Father's will and direction for our life. Yet God will help us to overcome and guide us through every obstacle when we seek Him. He is a very present help in time of need. (Psalms 46:1). You can find the answers for every barrier in His Word.

The Unfamiliar Touch
(Lessons from the woman with the issue of Blood)

- **Listening to God**

Giving attention to the Lord's direction is essential to breaking through the barriers in live. If you do not discern and obey His voice, you will follow the voice of a stranger and miss your breakthrough.
Get in the habit of listening and instantly obeying the voice of the Lord.

- **Keeping your focus on Jesus, not the barrier**

This is essential to overcoming every negative situation. Don't be problem focused. Focus on the promises in His Word. Knowing that God is with you and will never forsake you will help you have the confidence to face every obstacle with hope and perseverance.

- **Rehearsing God's victories**

Psalm 63:7-8 tell us, *"Because you are my help, I sing in the shadow of Your wings. My soul clings to You; Your right hand upholds me"*.

It's important to remember all the ways the Lord has helped you and delivered you in the past so you can remain encouraged in the face of every obstacle.

- **Staying in faith**

Faith is the opposite of fear. Fear attracts the very thing we fear. (Job said *"that which I feared has come upon me"*). Faith is what overcomes

The Unfamiliar Touch
(Lessons from the woman with the issue of Blood)

and brings victory. (1John 5:4) When you face every challenge with faith, you will be unstoppable! Champions meet every challenge with faith.

The only way you lose is to give up. *"Don't grow weary in doing good, for at the proper time we will reap a harvest if we do not give up." (Galatians 6:9).* It takes perseverance to overcome. It is through faith and patience we inherit the promises of God. Don't let the devil discourage you into giving up. Trust in God. He is able to put you through.

God is absolutely faithful in keeping His promises. So as you are confronted by barriers in life, commit yourself to overcoming them by identifying them, seeking God, listening to His instructions,

The Unfamiliar Touch
(Lessons from the woman with the issue of Blood)

maintaining your focus on Him, recalling His faithfulness in the past, keeping in faith and never ever giving up. Your heavenly Father wants the very best for you, and He will help you overcome every barrier.

- **Rebuke**

How do we define rebuke? We commonly think of rebuke as an adverse confrontation, but Proverbs 27:5-6 says, *"Better is open rebuke than hidden love. Wounds from a friend can be trusted, but an enemy multiplies kisses."*

The word Reprehension, or rebuke, can be a verb, meaning to sternly reprimand or scold, but it can also be a noun, because a rebuke is the result of being scolded. The root comes from the Old French *Rebuchier* and

The Unfamiliar Touch
(Lessons from the woman with the issue of Blood)

means "to hack down," or "beat back." A rebuke, then, is meant to be critical and to chide — in today's terms, a rebuke is verbal smack-down.

To rebuke someone is to criticize him or her pointedly, for a particular observed sinful behavior. The Greek word most often translated as "rebuke" in the New Testament is *Elegchó*. In its most comprehensive understanding, elegchó means "to reprimand and convict by exposing (sometimes publicly) a wrong." There are moments when we all should be rebuked if we fall into sin, and there are times when a believer needs to rebuke another believer with love and discernment.

The Unfamiliar Touch
(Lessons from the woman with the issue of Blood)

Jesus gave explicit directions for managing situations in which a fellow Christian is engaging in a sin: *"If your brother or sister sins, go and point out their fault, just between the two of you. If they listen to you, you have won them over" (Matthew 18:15).*

We all sin in many ways, but when another believer is choosing sin that harms themself, someone else, or the body of Christ, we are to intervene.

A rebuke is needed at times, as we must care for each other and live in truth. *James 5:20 says, "Whoever turns a sinner from the error of their way will save them from death and cover over a multitude of sins."*

A confrontation may be difficult, but it is not loving to allow a self-proclaimed Christian to proceed in a

The Unfamiliar Touch
(Lessons from the woman with the issue of Blood)

sin that will bring God's judgment upon them or their family.

We as Christians, shouldn't fear reprehension, the woman with the issue of blood had to get pass the possibility of rebuke, she had to get pass the possibility of being criticized publicly and in doing so, received her healing.

> **A rebuke is needed at times, as we must care for each other and live in truth.**

- **We are for signs and wonders**

Isaiah 8:18 KJV "Behold, I and the children whom the LORD hath given me are for signs and for wonders in Israel from the LORD of hosts, which dwelleth in mount Zion."

The Unfamiliar Touch
(Lessons from the woman with the issue of Blood)

A sign is an event, pattern that conveys a meaning or shows that an event is taking place.

While a wonder is a miraculous deed or event that cause surprise or admiration; a thing that makes people to come and see.

So signs and wonders simply refers to experiences that are perceived to be miraculous as being normative in the modern Christian experience, and is a phrase associated with groups that are a part of modern charismatic movements and Pentecostalism.

God is the Provider of signs and wonders (Isaiah 7:14). It proves that as God was with the Jews in the Old Testament, so God is still the same, He does not change.

The Unfamiliar Touch
(Lessons from the woman with the issue of Blood)

As human beings, no-one is born into any family by accident. God clearly chooses the family for us to be born into, because He definitely has a purpose for our lives. As children of God, we are for sign and wonder to our generation (Isaiah 8:18).

Many signs and wonders were recorded in the Old Testament, from the time Sarah gave birth to Isaac in her old age (Genesis 21:1-4); Moses parting of the Red sea with his rod (Exodus 14:21-31); Joshua commanding the Sun to stand still until the people had avenged themselves (Joshua 10:12-14), to the New Testament which is all about Jesus' ministry.

The Unfamiliar Touch
(Lessons from the woman with the issue of Blood)

Jesus performed many wonders and miracles before He died on the cross for our sins; like changing water into wine (John 2:1-11); walking on the water (Matthew 14:22-33); feeding the multitude (Matthew 14:15-21); Lazarus resurrecting from the dead (John 11:); to Jesus' disciples, who also performed many miracles.

As Christians, we must rely on God's miracles and stand firm in our faith. Faith makes us believe that with God, all things are possible. Elijah withheld rain for over three years, we can also do that. When we are filled with the power of the Holy Spirit, we will be able to cast out demons using God's Word and they will obey (Psalm 18:44).

The Unfamiliar Touch
(Lessons from the woman with the issue of Blood)

No matter the situation or circumstances, let us rejoice because God created us with a divine purpose that works to overcome any situations.

God is omnipresent. He has no limits and performs signs and wonders in our present time. Through the help of the Holy Spirit, God will perform signs and wonders that will give us testimonies and at the end of the day. Furthermore, God will be glorified in our lives for His sovereign power working in us. Stay connected to Jesus who is highly exalted by God and every tongue will confess that Jesus Christ is Lord, to the glory of God the Father, (Philippians 2: 9-11). For those yet to surrender their lives to Jesus, this is nonnegotiable, do so now, tomorrow might be too late so DO IT NOW!

The Unfamiliar Touch
(Lessons from the woman with the issue of Blood)

So from this chapter, we can learn the importance of prayer and why we need it in our lives. We can also learn the ways and virtues in which we can utilize to achieve our breakthroughs, however, there are more and we shall discuss them in the subsequent chapters. We shall all be for signs and wonders in the mighty name of Jesus. Amen.

The Unfamiliar Touch
(Lessons from the woman with the issue of Blood)

Chapter Five

Nothing to Lose

Introduction

In this chapter, we shall discuss the remarkable level of perseverance exhibited by the woman with the issue of blood and why we should aspire to achieve such. Furthermore, we shall discuss faith and the impact of making resolutions.

Persistence

To be persistent means being tenacious or determined. It means to continue in the course of an action irrespective of difficulties in life.

The Unfamiliar Touch
(Lessons from the woman with the issue of Blood)

People often give up because a request is "repeated."

The requester cannot allow themselves to become discouraged merely because their first or second request is denied. They must be persistent. The Greek word translated as *"persistence"* means *"shameless,"* suggesting freedom from the bashfulness that would stop a person from asking a second time. Knocking once does not indicate perseverance, but "continued" knocking does.

So put simply, persistence means quietly and steadily continuing a task despite any or many difficulties.

God often answers us after long and persevering requests. He hears prayers and grants blessings long after they appear to be unanswered or withheld.

The Unfamiliar Touch
(Lessons from the woman with the issue of Blood)

He does not promise to give blessings immediately. He promises only that He will do it according to His will and plan. Although He promises to answer the prayer of the faithful, often He requires us to wait a long time to test our faith. He may allow us to persevere for months or even years, until we are completely dependent on Him, until we see that there is no other way to receive the blessing, and until we are prepared to receive it. Sometimes, we are not ready to receive a blessing when we first ask. We may be too proud, or we may not comprehend our dependence upon Him. Perhaps we wouldn't value it, or the timing for it may simply be wrong. If what we ask for is good and accords with God's will, He will give it at the best time possible.

The Unfamiliar Touch
(Lessons from the woman with the issue of Blood)

So we must knock. We must persevere, we must be persistent, we must press the matter until we receive it (Hebrews 4:16).

We should faithfully go to God repeatedly, until He responds to our prayers and grants what we ask of Him—if it is according to His will. Like he did with Veronica. She would not let the Levitical laws, her pains or feebleness stop her. She made no excuse. Some people are one excuse away from their miracle(s).

The woman with the issue of blood took that bold step by being persistent in life and that is what many of us in this our current age must learnt to cultivate in life.

The Unfamiliar Touch
(Lessons from the woman with the issue of Blood)

> *Persistence means quietly and steadily continuing a task despite any or many difficulties*

Resolution

Simply put, resolution or spiritual goals, are the objectives we set for ourselves to get closer to God. Why do we need spiritual goals? We may have different religious beliefs but if there's one thing that binds us all, it's the thirst for spiritual nourishment.

While most of us go to church, recite prayers and take part in various spiritual rites, most of the time this isn't enough to fill that void inside us. That void that causes us to crave for a deeper connection with ourselves and our creator.

The Unfamiliar Touch
(Lessons from the woman with the issue of Blood)

This is what spiritual goals are for. It helps us grow and mature spiritually and build a better relationship with God and our fellows. It also grants us the mental preparation in accordance with or pending breakthroughs. And just like the woman with the issue of blood, who made a firm decision and set spiritual goals, we must also make our bold and definite resolutions no matter the circumstances. God didn't fail her, so he most definitely won't fail us. Furthermore, some examples of spiritual goals include:

- **Actively taking part in church services**

Attending it is not enough. You need to be in there physically, mentally and spiritually.

The Unfamiliar Touch
(Lessons from the woman with the issue of Blood)

- **Practicing forgiveness**

Forgiving someone who has wronged you will not only heal relationships. It will give you peace of mind too.

- **Charity**

Doing charity should not only be confined to Christmas and Thanksgiving alone. Giving back or charity should be done all year round. Strive to be a blessing to others every single day and the Lord will surely reward you.

- **Reading inspirational books**

Aside from the bible, inspirational books are a great way to attain spiritual fulfillment.

The Unfamiliar Touch
(Lessons from the woman with the issue of Blood)

- **Conversing with God daily**

Endeavour to find a few minutes each day to spend alone with God. Tell him about the things you're thankful for each day as well as the things that you're worried about. Talk to him as you would a friend. He'll surely listen to you.

- **Power of Faith**

Faith is synonymous with the word "Believe". To believe is to accept the fact that something is true or possible, especially without proof. She believed that touching His garment will make her whole even though she had no proof anyone had been healed by touching His garment before. The woman with the issue of blood believed in Jesus and in His ability to

The Unfamiliar Touch
(Lessons from the woman with the issue of Blood)

heal even when His garment is touched. She believed that touching Jesus would make her whole.

There is an undeniable fact that we all know to be true, and that is God gives us power when we make right choices.

When we choose to live our lives in accordance with His word, His will, and His way; then we'll have additional power for life.

God uses all kinds of people with different backgrounds, and of various ages, economic and social status, languages, and ethnicity. In other words, God uses people who are not afraid to trust him completely, or what we call as having faith, and this faith produces enormous power for greater purpose. What the Bible tells us is that there is a direct correlation

The Unfamiliar Touch
(Lessons from the woman with the issue of Blood)

between faith and power. The more faith we put in God, the more we allow God to direct our lives, the more power and blessing we're going to have.

We see this correlation when Jesus visits His hometown of Nazareth.

> *"He did not do many mighty works there because of their unbelief." (Matthew 13:58)*

Notice the connection between power and faith. It was their unbelief and lack of faith that stopped Jesus' power from manifesting greatly there.

Furthermore, the Bible tells us that Abraham was the father of faith, and God's commentary on Abraham's life shows us why:

The Unfamiliar Touch
(Lessons from the woman with the issue of Blood)

"He did not waver at the promise of God through unbelief, but was strengthened in faith, giving glory to God." (Romans 4:20)

God never meant for any of us to go through life in this world alone, that is, in our own power and understanding. God has unlimited power just waiting and available for us to harness, and the results are enormous amounts of energy that we never thought possible. The woman with the issue of blood, through her faith and determination, tapped into this divine source of power and received her divine healing and medical breakthrough.

So we can conclude that from the chapter above, Faith and perseverance are two powerful virtues we much

The Unfamiliar Touch
(Lessons from the woman with the issue of Blood)

possess if we aspire to claim our miracles.

However, to achieve this, we must also work, for faith without work is dead.

Veronica had faith, she believed in her healing, but she still had certain tasks to accomplish before she could be healed. We shall discuss these in Chapters six and seven.

The Unfamiliar Touch
(Lessons from the woman with the issue of Blood)

Chapter Six

Divine Idea 1 - Disguise

Introduction

In this chapter, we shall discuss an idea she conceived that was of critical importance in receiving her miracle. This seemingly elementary idea, was no doubt, a divine inspiration that was necessary for her miracle. This idea is that of "disguise", and in this chapter, we shall shed more light on it.

Its meaning

Put simply, an idea is an aim, a purpose, a thought or suggestion as to a possible course of action. While to disguise means to deliberately alter the dress or appearance of something,

The Unfamiliar Touch
(Lessons from the woman with the issue of Blood)

someone or oneself, so as to conceal the identity or true nature.

A disguise implies a change in appearance or behavior that usually misleads by presenting a different apparent identity.

Its significance

The significance of spiritual disguises are usually to conceal our blessings and breakthroughs through the manifestation of seemingly unfavorable circumstances and situations till they are most needed. This is commonly known as *"blessings in disguise."*

Her need for such

She had ideas for her own miracle. She presumably heard how the paralytic was healed by breaking the

The Unfamiliar Touch
(Lessons from the woman with the issue of Blood)

roof and was helped by four of his friends. So she must have said to herself, "since I am unclean and no one would help me.

I may have to disguise myself and possibly kneel and crawl if I have to".

It was recorded that she became part of the crowd in a somewhat disguised state, in other words, her clothing (because of her condition) may have been layered, and she may have covered her face fully so as not to be seen or recognised. Although the book of Mark recounts specific details about the woman and her unsuccessful search amongst doctors for a cure, it remains silent about something every other woman who hears or reads the story realises:

The Unfamiliar Touch
(Lessons from the woman with the issue of Blood)

The woman's life was a constant routine of washing and drying rags to catch and staunch the flow of her blood. Furthermore, her condition would have most likely emitted an odour.

As such, it is potentially very embarrassing. Significantly, her condition excludes her from worship and community life. Concerning the fact that first century life stresses the importance of congregational worship in a synagogue and the communal value of praying and responding together.

Therefore, a woman with the ongoing condition of unstoppable menstrual flow would be a tremendous burden on her family. All garments, linens, utensils, and furniture she touched, sat

The Unfamiliar Touch
(Lessons from the woman with the issue of Blood)

on or used had to be washed. Likewise, people who touched her were unclean until evening.

Evidently, eventually her prolonged condition seems to have led to her exclusion from her family, for the Bible says she had spent all her money on a worthless chase of healing from physicians who only increased her suffering (Mark 5:26).

I imagine her life as one without hugs from friends, children and parents, as lacking normal human contact, as devoid of marital rights with its duties and privileges, as full of toil because of the need to constantly wash everything, and as expensive because of the financial implications of a chronic illness. She was probably without income, because she would

The Unfamiliar Touch
(Lessons from the woman with the issue of Blood)

have been unemployable. In a Jewish culture dominated by the shame and/or honour motif, the woman experienced numerous embarrassment and exclusion.

All these logical factors unquestionably lead to this reasonable conclusion: that this woman was lonely, isolated, impoverished, probably anaemic and possibly dying. Furthermore, her condition appeared hopeless and she was definitely desperate. Quite a large number of people would think that she was better off dead.

Its reward

Mark 5:29 KJV "And straightway the fountain of her blood was dried up; and she felt in her body that she was healed of that plague."

The Unfamiliar Touch
(Lessons from the woman with the issue of Blood)

The book of Mark 5:29 says that she felt in her body that she was healed. Not many people can sense this tangible anointing unless there was a powerful presence of the Holy Spirit moving at that moment. In her case the Bible says she could sense that she was healed and made whole instantly.

Here is something we all need to understand. God can only meet us at the level of our expectancy. And this woman was in absolute expectation for a miracle in her life.

This concludes the importance of spiritual perceptiveness and divine inspiration, a seemingly simple form of disguise paved way for her miracle. Similar instances and circumstances that requires divine inspiration to unlock our breakthroughs, could be

The Unfamiliar Touch
(Lessons from the woman with the issue of Blood)

going on in our everyday lives but we may fail to realize them. I pray that in this hour, our perceptiveness for divine inspiration be opened in the mighty name of Jesus. Amen.

The Unfamiliar Touch
(Lessons from the woman with the issue of Blood)

Chapter Seven

Divine Idea II – His Garment

Introduction

This is a continuation of the previous chapter which discussed her first idea, known as disguise.

In this chapter, we shall discuss the second, which involved the garment of Jesus. Furthermore, we shall shed more light on the word "Garment" itself and grasp its physical and spiritual meaning and significance.

Its meaning

The word "Garment" is derived from the French word for "equipment," garment is a somewhat generic term

The Unfamiliar Touch
(Lessons from the woman with the issue of Blood)

you can use when the specific kind of clothing you're describing is not the point.

A dress, for example, is a dress, trousers are trousers and underclothes are underclothes. They are not the same thing, unless you refer to them both as garments, in which case they are the same thing.

The clothing of the people in Biblical times was made from wool, linen, animal skins, and perhaps silk. Most events in the Old and New Testament take place in ancient Israel, and thus most Biblical clothing is ancient Hebrew clothing. They wore underwear and cloth skirts.

The Unfamiliar Touch
(Lessons from the woman with the issue of Blood)

Its significance

Biblically, a person's garment signifies their spiritual status and authority. Spiritually, everyone is considered to be clothed with one form of garment or the other.

A major example of this can be found in (Zechariah 3:1-5): *Zechariah 3:1-5 KJV*

(1) And he shewed me Joshua the high priest standing before the angel of the LORD, and Satan standing at his right hand to resist him.

(2) And the LORD said unto Satan, The LORD rebuke thee, O Satan; even the LORD that hath chosen Jerusalem rebuke thee: is not this a brand plucked out of the fire?

The Unfamiliar Touch
(Lessons from the woman with the issue of Blood)

(3) Now Joshua was clothed with filthy garments, and stood before the angel.

(4) And he answered and spake unto those that stood before him, saying, Take away the filthy garments from him. And unto him he said, Behold, I have caused thine iniquity to pass from thee, and I will clothe thee with change of raiment.

(5) And I said, Let them set a fair mitre upon his head. So they set a fair mitre upon his head, and clothed him with garments. And the angel of the LORD stood by."

The scripture above reveals that Joshua the high priest was physically clothed with a dignifying priestly garment to carry out his assignment, however in the spiritual realm, he wore a filthy garment. Holiness and

The Unfamiliar Touch
(Lessons from the woman with the issue of Blood)

purity is usually represented by a White garment.

So it is important therefore, to note that what we are wearing spiritually is far more significant than what we are wearing physically. Furthermore, a garment signifies many things examples are:

Identity

garment signifies identity. For example, when you see a nurse in uniform, you instantly know who he or she is.

- **Authority:**

A person's garment signifies their authority. The level of authority or a soldier's rank is confirmed by the stripes and/or stars on his or her uniform.

The Unfamiliar Touch
(Lessons from the woman with the issue of Blood)

- **Dignity:**

Garment signifies dignity. A well-dressed individual is considered a dignified person while a shabbily dressed person loses respect before people.

- **Status and Prosperity:**

We can usually identify a wealthy person by what they wear most times, depicting that he or she is a prosperous person.

The unfamiliar touch

The Unfamiliar touch is an uncommon, unconventional and unique kind of touch. It is a different kind of touch. It is Intentional and directional. It is calculated and done to provoke something in another person. It is done to arouse or draw attention. It is done to kindle a kind of

The Unfamiliar Touch
(Lessons from the woman with the issue of Blood)

feeling or response from another person. It is purposeful, that is, it is full of purpose. It is done with a reason. And most importantly, It has the potential to produce uncommon miracles.

Mark 5:30KJV "And Jesus, immediately knowing in himself that virtue had gone out of him, turned him about in the press, and said, Who touched my clothes?"

Since there are references in the gospels (such as Matthew 9:4 or Matthew 12:25) to Jesus knowing people's thoughts, this implies that the referenced verse does not reflect a lack of omniscience on Jesus' part. Put simply, Jesus certainly knew who had touched Him. However, Jesus asked that question for the purpose of having the woman who had been

The Unfamiliar Touch
(Lessons from the woman with the issue of Blood)

healed provide a witness of both her personal faith and her healing to the crowds that surrounded him.

Jesus didn't have to acknowledge the woman. Her faith to touch the hem of his garment was enough to heal her. It seems that he wanted to look her in the eye, not to rebuke her for touching him, but to see the beautiful, genuine faith emanating from her heart. He wanted to acknowledge that she didn't have to suffer anymore. She was finally free.

Physical healings don't always happen, but sometimes they do. So ask and keep on asking with the faith and determination of the dear woman in this story. But even when there isn't physical healing, there will always be healing of your heart and

The Unfamiliar Touch
(Lessons from the woman with the issue of Blood)

soul when you repent of doing things your way and thank God for making a way for your sin, shame, and pride to be completely covered. You can be free. He will say, "Daughter (or Son), your faith has healed you. Go in peace and be freed from your suffering."

Ways to touch Jesus

Touching Jesus is a deliberate action, it is a purposeful action. When Andrew and another disciple of John the Baptist started following Jesus, the first thing he asked them was their purpose. He asked: *"what do you seek"* (John 1:37-40)? They answered: *"where you dwell"*. Then he granted their request saying: *"come and see"*; he invited them to a new experience of himself.

The Unfamiliar Touch
(Lessons from the woman with the issue of Blood)

You touch Jesus to tap from his virtue, to get some of what he is full of. John wrote that he is full of grace and truth. He also wrote that in him was life. Below are ways in which we can touch Jesus:

- **Giving your life to him**

When you give your life to Jesus, this touches his heart and moves him to give the gift of his Holy Spirit to live in your heart. The Holy Spirit will be your counselor, your guide, your strength, your friend, your defender and your peace in troubled times. We can achieve this by helping people in need and seeking forgiveness for our sins. So endeavour to make Jesus Christ the center of your life and ask him to help you do his will each day. When you pray, believe in your heart

The Unfamiliar Touch
(Lessons from the woman with the issue of Blood)

that God has heard your prayer and pray that God's will be done, not yours.

- **Becoming a soul winner**

The term "soul-winner" is used metaphorically for evangelism. To be a soul-winner refers to the practice of teaching a lost sinner the good news about Christ. Soul winning is an important part of Christianity. And we must attend to it if we want to please God and enjoy the benefits of soul winning that He has for us. So every Christian is expected to be a soul winner.

- **His Word**

The Word of God is the manifestation of the mind and will of God. It is the

The Unfamiliar Touch
(Lessons from the woman with the issue of Blood)

Holy Bible and the preaching of Christ, and we as Christians should endeavour to study it regularly.

When we read and meditate on his Word, we establish a connection between ourselves and Jesus as this act of solemn and devoted worship touches his heart and draws him closer to us.

Our Faith

Faith is simply the assurance of things hoped for, the conviction of things not seen. One of the most potent ways of touching Jesus is through our faith. Through faith, you can lay hold of Jesus right now—irrespective of how unclean you might feel—and experience the same power the woman with the issue of blood did. As a matter of fact, her healing didn't come simply because she touched

The Unfamiliar Touch
(Lessons from the woman with the issue of Blood)

Jesus because many in the crowd had done this, but because she touched him with faith.

Mark 5:34 KJV And he said unto her, Daughter, thy faith hath made thee whole; go in peace, and be whole of thy plague.

- **Our Works**

In Christian theology, good works, or simply works, are a person's (exterior) actions or deeds, in contrast to inner qualities such as grace or faith. Faith without work is dead, so our good deeds are as important as our faith if we aspire to touch Jesus. So to serve God is to serve others and that is the greatest form of charity, which is the pure love of Christ, as Jesus said in

John 13:34KJV A new commandment I give unto you, That ye love one

The Unfamiliar Touch
(Lessons from the woman with the issue of Blood)

another; as I have loved you, that ye also love one another.

- **Giving**

Giving is actually a deeply personal indicator of our spiritual maturity as well as our love for God. An amazing benefit of giving is that it releases us from the real burden of our own financial needs.

So as we learn to trust God through giving, we can live confidently on what is left because we know that God is taking care of that. Giving is a liberating experience as it connects us more closely to God relationally. When we give to charity, the widows, widowers and the less privileged wholeheartedly, giving then becomes worship. It becomes a way of saying

The Unfamiliar Touch
(Lessons from the woman with the issue of Blood)

thanks to God for His grace and promised provision. Giving becomes a deep part of our personal connection to God.

> **When we give to charity, the widows, widowers and the less privileged wholeheartedly, giving then becomes worship.**

So in conclusion, we can verify the critical importance of receiving divine inspiration and the roles they play in receiving our miraculous breakthroughs. The woman with the issue of blood, through faith and prayer, was spiritually perceptive and this paved the way for her miracles.

The Unfamiliar Touch
(Lessons from the woman with the issue of Blood)

I pray that we receive the same spiritual grace in the mighty name of Jesus. Amen.

Chapter Eight

The woman with the issue of blood – Lessons

Introduction

In this chapter, we shall discuss the numerous lessons learned from the story of the woman with the issue of blood and how we can integrate them to our daily lives.

The Unfamiliar Touch
(Lessons from the woman with the issue of Blood)

She heard the word of God.

It is significant that the woman had heard about Jesus as recorded in Mark 5:27. The definite article before the name Jesus in verse 27 indicates there was a specific Jesus amongst many of that name of whom she had heard. But what exactly had she heard?

The book of Mark seems to indicate she had heard the earlier stories and preachings in his narrative, thus hearing the word of God.

Several times we overlook the fact that God speaks to us all the time, we may not even know it and we don't give Him the credit. So listen to that voice! He will always give you peace. He also will never contradict His written word in the Bible.

The Unfamiliar Touch
(Lessons from the woman with the issue of Blood)

Ideas

Her two major ideas were centred on her disguise and the touching of Jesus's garment. Both were critically important and each played a role in her divine healing.

First, if she hadn't disguised herself, she would most likely have been recognized by someone and her intentions would have eventually come into light. This would have greatly reduced her chances of encountering Jesus.

Second, her need to touch his garment. Due to the crowd and the large number of people that were surrounding Jesus, she probably wouldn't have gotten his attention, not to mention her divine healing. These ideas she conceived enabled her to

The Unfamiliar Touch
(Lessons from the woman with the issue of Blood)

"claim" her miracle through Faith rather than supplication. So put simply, she could not throw herself, therefore, at the feet of Christ and state her complaint. Her modesty, humility, uncleanness and pressure of the crowd made close contact nearly impossible, hence her eagerness to touch in some unnoticed way the hem of His garment.

We should endeavour to be spiritually perceptive and attentive if we are to claim our miracles, breakthroughs and divine healing.

She put faith into action

The crowd who listened to her confession also heard the Saviour's benediction, *"Daughter, be of good comfort; thy faith hath saved thee; go in peace."* As a true daughter of

The Unfamiliar Touch
(Lessons from the woman with the issue of Blood)

Abraham (Luke 13:16), her faith is crowned by the Master. Hers was not faith without a touch, or a touch without faith. Her faith was definitely acted upon and the results surely didn't disappoint her.

Decision

By the time the woman had gotten to Jesus, He was busy and surrounded by a crowd of people. Jarius, the most important man in the community, had summoned him to help his daughter and Jesus was in route. Definitely her window of opportunity was closing quickly and what little hope she had was fading. This woman was certainly down to her last prayer and she prayed it. What were the odds that Jesus would interrupt an urgent

The Unfamiliar Touch
(Lessons from the woman with the issue of Blood)

mission with an important official to help her? Very few. But twelve years is a long time and what are the odds that she would survive if she didn't take a chance? Fewer still. Her back was up against the wall and against all odds... so she stepped out on faith and took a chance.

She was thinking to herself, *"If I can put a finger on his robe, I can get well."* It was clearly a risky decision. To touch Jesus she had to touch the people. To get to Jesus she had to get pass the roadblocks. She had to get pass the possibility of rebuke, she had to get pass the possibility of being recognized. But what choice does she have? Her decision turned out to be the right one. Obviously, exercising Faith means you must be willing to take some risk

The Unfamiliar Touch
(Lessons from the woman with the issue of Blood)

She knelt down - Position of Prayer

The woman with the issue of blood knelt down to pray. Now Kneeling may not be necessary to reverent adoration, but it does promote a proper attitude. God is holy and we are not. But on a more positive note, supplicants often kneel while praying as a sign of humble submission before the Lord. In the Old Testament, one of the psalmists enjoins us, *"Oh come, let us worship and bow down; let us kneel before the Lord, our Maker!" (Psalm 95:6).* When offering prayers of forgiveness and supplications onto God, we should endeavour to display humility and submission to ensure the speedy acknowledgement of our prayers.

The Unfamiliar Touch
(Lessons from the woman with the issue of Blood)

She prostrated - Position of Worship - Warships for Welfare

Prostration is the placement of the body in a reverentially or submissively prone position as a gesture. Typically prostration is distinguished from the lesser acts of bowing or kneeling by involving a part of the body above the knee touching the ground, especially the hands.

With respect to the Bible, prostration is usually synonymous with worship.

However, that relationship can come only from the heart of a person – one's spirit. It can only exist if it is truthful in all aspects with the Creator. We are now able to worship our God in spirit and truth because the Truth, Jesus, has been revealed to us. Our worship

The Unfamiliar Touch
(Lessons from the woman with the issue of Blood)

always radiates from Him. Furthermore, when we worship the Lord wholeheartedly, he prepares "Warships that go into Warfare for our welfare". In other words, he will fight our battles and protect us provided our faith in him is resolute.

So in conclusion, we can learn the numerous morals or lessons discussed in this chapter.

Furthermore, we can also learn the significance of certain actions, like prayer and worship and their potential when seeking divine favour. I pray that we receive the wisdom, knowledge and understanding to incorporate these into our lives in the mighty name of Jesus. Amen.

The Unfamiliar Touch
(Lessons from the woman with the issue of Blood)

She crawled - Position of Perseverance - Overcoming offense

Spiritually, crawling may seem to signify experiencing embarrassment or desperation in your life, but this however, is not always the case. Crawling can also be a sign of persevering growth and development if you are moving towards something you desire in your dream or vision. Crawling can also indicate uncertainty and discomfort in a new situation in your life. You might have a while to go before you are going to be comfortable with a new situation that you have found yourself in. So dreaming that you are crawling slow towards something can indicate the need to work hard in order to achieve specific goals in your life. You might desire instant success, however, the

The Unfamiliar Touch
(Lessons from the woman with the issue of Blood)

reality is you will still need to work hard in one way or the other through faith, and be dedicated to achieve your desired goals in life. Crawling may also depict humility and meekness.

The woman with the issue of blood was led by the Holy Spirit to position herself to crawl into the presence of God and touch the bottom of His garment. However, this in itself was surely not an easy task as there was such a crowd that she literally had to push through and crawl on all fours and even on her belly, all in order to get close enough to Jesus. While doing this, she was offensively pushed, shoved, kicked and stepped on all over. But she didn't relent nor pay the crowd any heed, her focus was on getting to Jesus.

The Unfamiliar Touch
(Lessons from the woman with the issue of Blood)

The significance of the above paragraph protrays that whenever we are close to obtaining our miracle(s), offenses can arise with the purpose of distracting us, leading us astray or tempting us to sin by violently retaliating or lashing out. Furthermore, these offenses may arise from anyone and at anywhere as depicted in the story of Hannah in 1 Samuel 1:12-15, which reads:

1 Samuel 1:12-15 KJV And it came to pass, as she continued praying before the LORD, that Eli marked her mouth. (13) Now Hannah, she spake in her heart; only her lips moved, but her voice was not heard: therefore Eli thought she had been drunken.
(14) And Eli said unto her, How long wilt thou be drunken? put away thy wine from thee.

The Unfamiliar Touch
(Lessons from the woman with the issue of Blood)

(15) And Hannah answered and said, No, my lord, I am a woman of a sorrowful spirit: I have drunk neither wine nor strong drink, but have poured out my soul before the LORD.

This brings us to the conclusion of this chapter. In the next chapter, we shall discuss disappointment and ways to endure and overcome it.

The Unfamiliar Touch
(Lessons from the woman with the issue of Blood)

Chapter Nine

Disappointment to This Appointment

Introduction

In this chapter, we shall discuss and shed light on the word "disappointment". We shall also discuss how to overcome it.

Its meaning

Disappointment, or to be disappointed, is defined as a feeling of sadness, dissatisfaction or displeasure when something isn't as you planned. It also means an act (or failure to act) that disappoints someone.

The Unfamiliar Touch
(Lessons from the woman with the issue of Blood)

Do not despair

The woman with the issue of blood did not allow her previous disappointments or the Levitical laws about uncleanliness to deter her from her receiving her deliverance.

The woman with the issue of blood never succumbed to despair despite all the disappointment she had faced. For the twelve years she suffered, she never gave up, she had wasted money on various physicians yet she didn't give up but kept her faith and zeal in God.

That is why every believer in Christ must always have faith as well in God and never give up on their faith. We must aspire to never be disappointed in life.

The Unfamiliar Touch
(Lessons from the woman with the issue of Blood)

Giving up in life must never be our priority because of disappointment. We may face a lot of problems in life. Sometimes we may be hurt both physically and emotionally, or disturbed because of the evil things that occurs in our lives but that is when we need to hold on to God the most.

Sometimes we would be disappointed, betrayed and even hurt by our loved ones but patience is the key to success. Nothing must stop us from shinning in life because even the disappointments, betrayals and shame we face may end up working for our own good and that is when God steps into our lives. Anytime we give our all to God and believe in Him for the best, He give us the best.

The Unfamiliar Touch
(Lessons from the woman with the issue of Blood)

God is with us and God wants the best for us and that is why we need to keep believing in God and serving Him at all cost.

Disappointment can affect our ministry and the things we do for God in life, and that is why we must never give up on something we really want, it's difficult to wait but it's more difficult to regret. If you feel like giving up, just look back on how far you have come already. Before you give up, think of the reason why you held on for so long.

Our hope must be built up in the Lord and we must hold on to Him in all we do and never give up in life because God has a plan for us all. God has a great plan for us and we need to seek Him in all that we do in this world.

The Unfamiliar Touch
(Lessons from the woman with the issue of Blood)

The woman with the issue of blood never gave up in life because she felt disappointed. We must also never give up in life because of disappointment and we must never lose the faith and zeal we have in God.

> **Sometimes we would be disappointed, betrayed and even hurt by our loved ones but patience is the key to success.**

God has a purpose for each and every one in life and there's a plan that God has set for everyone. We must never give up in life, and we must never lose hope in life, because there are greater plans God has for each and every one of us.

Giving up because of disappointment doesn't solve the problem because we

The Unfamiliar Touch
(Lessons from the woman with the issue of Blood)

must know that we can only do all things through Christ who strengthens us. God wants us to stay steadfast in Him and serve Him in faithfulness and that is why we need to believe in the power of God and serve Him with all our might.

So let's keep being strong and let's not give up in life because God wants to expand the calling He has for us and the things He wants to do in our lives. Giving up because of disappointment can create a lot of problems for us because our issues may end up increasing.

Anytime God lifts us up, he prepares something greater for us. Many people have given up because they are disappointed and they haven't been able to succeed in life ever since. The

The Unfamiliar Touch
(Lessons from the woman with the issue of Blood)

woman with the issue of blood never gave up on life and that is how she was able to make it in life.

We must never give up in life because of disappointment. The Lord God is our strength, shield, and in him alone we can trust. God has called us to do greater things in life.

Out of her disappointment God appointed her, and took her into her next level as she was transformed.

God will definitely turn your disappointments into His appointments for your appointments.

So in conclusion, disappointment is something that is never truly desired by anyone, but i believe that in this chapter, we overcame it. I pray that you shall also overcome every form

The Unfamiliar Touch
(Lessons from the woman with the issue of Blood)

of disappointment in the mighty name of Jesus. Amen.

We shall now move on to our last and final chapter, called "Seeking attention". What does this mean? Let's find out.

The Unfamiliar Touch
(Lessons from the woman with the issue of Blood)

Chapter Ten
Seeking attention

Introduction

In this final chapter, we shall shed light on seeking attention. We shall discuss its earthly and spiritual meaning, along with its importance and ways we can perform this.

Its meaning

Seeking attention can be defined as the exhibition of attention-seeking behavior which can include saying or doing something with the goal of getting the attention of a person or a group of people. Examples of this

The Unfamiliar Touch
(Lessons from the woman with the issue of Blood)

behavior include: fishing for compliments by pointing out achievements and seeking validation. Or being controversial to provoke a reaction.

Its significance

Spiritually, seeking God's attention is very important and significant, and this mainly involves praying for others. The reason why praying for others is one of the best ways to get God's attention is that, it is a form of sacrifice we make to God and sacrifice attracts the attention of God quickly. One of the things we do that touches the heart of God is our sacrifice for others. When we do for others we also do unto God.

The Unfamiliar Touch
(Lessons from the woman with the issue of Blood)

Why we need it

Jeremiah 29:13-14 KJV "And ye shall seek me, and find me, when ye shall search for me with all your heart.

(14) And I will be found of you, saith the LORD: and I will turn away your captivity, and I will gather you from all the nations, and from all the places whither I have driven you, saith the LORD; and I will bring you again into the place whence I caused you to be carried away captive."

We need to seek God's attention because he is the giver of life (1 Timothy 6:13; John 10:10). He is the great I AM (Exodus 3:14). In God we find purpose, meaning, and satisfaction. Humans were created for relationship with God and relationship with one another. If we do not seek

The Unfamiliar Touch
(Lessons from the woman with the issue of Blood)

God, how can we know Him? How will we experience the life He gives? Apart from seeking Him, how will we understand His great love and our purpose? Because of the graciousness of God and the gift of free will, God does not force Himself upon us.

He woos us to Himself. He pursues us, and we seek Him.

We seek God because He has invited us to do so. Knowing God is a privilege. We seek Him through prayer, Scripture reading, worship, and fellowship. In seeking God we come to know Him better and we bring Him glory

Its reward

God will verify that your drawing closer to Him will not be in vain. He too will take steps towards you.

The Unfamiliar Touch
(Lessons from the woman with the issue of Blood)

Approach God with a pure heart because He is holy and desires holiness in you. God knows we need His presence daily to feel His love, peace, protection, and care.

The great promise to those who seek the Lord is that he will be found. *"If you seek him, he will be found by you" (1 Chronicles 28:9).* And when he is found, there is great reward. *"Whoever would draw near to God must believe that he exists and that he rewards those who seek him" (Hebrews 11:6).*

His Will be done

Psalms 57:2 KJV "I will cry unto God most high; unto God that performeth all things for me."

Psalm 57:2 says, "I cry out to God Most High, to God who fulfills his

The Unfamiliar Touch
(Lessons from the woman with the issue of Blood)

purpose for me." This is key in understanding God's purpose for your life. God has numbered your days and will fulfill every purpose He has for you.

Life may be full of ups and downs. There shall be times we would want to give up in life, there would be times we would want to give up on our faith, there would be times we would decide not to trust in God again but we must learn to seek God in all we do, trust in Him and allow His will to be made manifested in our lives.

A lot of things may fight our destinies and future and try to stop us from becoming what God wants us to become in life and that is why we must learn to lean on God every day because he has a plan for us in life.

The Unfamiliar Touch
(Lessons from the woman with the issue of Blood)

There are a lot of things that would try to block our success, freedom, progress and even breakthrough in life and that is why we need to keep our focus on God.

> **God would work out more things in our lives if we keep trusting in Him and seeking Him.**

There are many things that are affecting us today and that is why we need to stay strong in God as always so that we can become better people in society.

The more we trust in God, the more he allows open doors in our lives.

God wants to elevate many of us to another level and that is why we need to become stronger in His word and

The Unfamiliar Touch
(Lessons from the woman with the issue of Blood)

allow the flow of His spirit to influence and rule our lives.

The woman with the issue of blood looked beyond her bad experiences and disappointments. She trusted in Jesus and she believed with Him all things would be possible.

We need to trust God for a miracle because there are greater things that the Lord is about to do in our lives and we would need more grace and power to work it out.

God would work out more things in our lives if we keep trusting in Him and seeking Him.

We need more power, more grace, more fire to be able to do exceedingly greater things for God.

The Unfamiliar Touch
(Lessons from the woman with the issue of Blood)

This is why despite the problems the woman with the issue of blood faced, she was able to master courage and she had wisdom to be able to discover her source of healing.

We must never give up on our calling, the faith we have in God, the destiny ahead of us, we must always trust God for the best in life so that God can open greater doors for us in life.

However, our choices and actions also really matter. Truth be told, In some ways, this is a mystery we can't fully understand, but that doesn't mean it's not true. We can choose to do things that will bring us more joy and give us more of a sense of purpose through Christ our strength. Amen.

In conclusion, seeking God's attention proves to be a very crucial act in

The Unfamiliar Touch
(Lessons from the woman with the issue of Blood)

receiving our divine blessing and healing. I pray that God gives us the strength and wisdom to never stop serving and searching for him, because once we do, then he'll never stop blessing us. May he bless you abundantly in the mighty name of Jesus. Amen.

So as we conclude this spiritual and educative book, I pray that the Lord imbibes us with the divine potential to actualize everything we have read for our Spiritual uplift, material blessings and to the Glory of his name. Amen.

The Unfamiliar Touch
(Lessons from the woman with the issue of Blood)

Prayer points

1. I am established in righteousness, and oppression is far from me, (Isaiah 54:14).
2. The weapons of my warfare are not carnal but mighty through God to the pulling down of strongholds, (second Corinthians 10:4).
3. I take the shield of faith, and I quench every fiery dart of the enemy, (Ephesians 6:16).
4. I take the sword of the Spirit, which is the Word of God, and use it against the enemy, (Ephesians 6:17).
5. I am redeemed from the curse of the law. I am redeemed from poverty. I am redeemed from sickness.

The Unfamiliar Touch
(Lessons from the woman with the issue of Blood)

6. I am redeemed from spiritual death, (Galatians 3:13).
7. I overcome all because greater is He that is in me than he that is in the world, (second John 4:4).
8. I stand in the evil day having my loins girded about with truth, and I have the breastplate of righteousness. My feet are shod with the gospel of peace. I take the shield of faith. I am covered with the helmet of salvation, and I use the sword of the Spirit, which is the Word of God, (Ephesians 6:14–17).
9. I am delivered from the power of darkness and translated into the kingdom of God's dear Son, (Colossians 1:13).

The Unfamiliar Touch
(Lessons from the woman with the issue of Blood)

10. I tread upon serpents and scorpions and over all the power of the enemy, and nothing shall hurt me, (Luke 10:19).
11. I do not have the spirit of fear but power, love, and a sound mind, (second Timothy 1:7).
12. I am blessed with all spiritual blessings in heavenly places in Christ Jesus, (Ephesians 1:3).
13. I am healed by the stripes of Jesus, (Isaiah 53:5).
14. My hand is upon the neck of my enemies, (Genesis 49:8).
15. You anoint my head with oil; my cup runs over. Goodness and mercy shall follow me all the days of my life, (Psalm 23:5–6).

The Unfamiliar Touch
(Lessons from the woman with the issue of Blood)

16. I am anointed to preach, to teach, to heal, and to cast out devils.
17. I receive abundance of grace and the gift of righteousness, and I reign in life through Christ Jesus, (Romans 5:17).
18. I have life and that more abundantly, (John 10:10).
19. I walk in the light as He is in the light, and the blood of Jesus cleanses me from all sin, (First John 1:7).
20. I am the righteousness of God in Christ, (Second Corinthians 5:21).
21. I am the head and not the tail, (Deuteronomy 28:13).
22. I shall decree a thing, and it shall be established in my life, (Job 22:28).

The Unfamiliar Touch
(Lessons from the woman with the issue of Blood)

23. I have favour with God and with man, (Luke 2:52).
24. Wealth and riches are in my house, and my righteousness endures forever, (Psalm 112:3). I will be satisfied with long life, and God will show me His salvation, (Psalm 91:16).
25. I dwell in the secret place of the Most High, and I abide under the shadow of the Almighty, (Psalm 91:1).
26. No evil will befall me, and no plague shall come near my dwelling, (Psalm 91:10).
27. My children are taught of the Lord, and great is their peace, (Isaiah 54:13).

The Unfamiliar Touch
(Lessons from the woman with the issue of Blood)

28. I am strengthened with might by His Spirit in the inner man, (Ephesians 3:16).
29. I am rooted and grounded in love, (Ephesians 3:17).
30. I bless my natural enemies, and I overcome evil with good, (Matthew 5:44).
31. No weapon formed against me shall prosper, and every tongue that rises against me in judgement, I condemn. (Isaiah 54:17)
32. Every negative issue in my life, I issue you with the certificate of termination.
33. Every issue swallowing up my true identity, vomit my identity now in Jesus name, amen.
34. Every issue mocking me, causing people to refer to me as

The Unfamiliar Touch
(Lessons from the woman with the issue of Blood)

that person with an issue of ………….(put the issues here) mock me no more in Jesus name.
35. Oh Lord, I touch you by faith now for my miracle in Jesus name, amen.
36. In the name of Jesus, I ask for and receive healing and deliverance from….(list the areas where you need

The Unfamiliar Touch
(Lessons from the woman with the issue of Blood)

Altar call to receive Christ

YOU CAN TOUCH JESUS NOW!

The greatest miracle is the miracle of salvation

One of the ways you can touch Jesus today is by surrendering your life to Him and accepting Him as your Lord and saviour.

If you would like to do so now, Kindly say this prayer with your whole heart.

Dear Lord Jesus Christ, Thank you for dying for the remission of my sins on the cross of Calvary.

I believe you are the son of God, that you died for my sins, were buried and rose on the third day and the you are

The Unfamiliar Touch
(Lessons from the woman with the issue of Blood)

seated at the right hand of Our father in heaven.

I believe you will come back again to take the saints to heaven.

With my heart I believe these things and that you are my Lord and personal Saviour.

Please forgive me my sins and I also forgive others right now because you first forgave me and if I don't forgive, you won't forgive me either. Write my name in the book of life.

Come into my life and become my Lord and personal saviour.

With my mouth I confess that you are my Lord and saviour of my soul

The Unfamiliar Touch
(Lessons from the woman with the issue of Blood)

Fill me with your Holy Spirit and grant me the grace to lead a life righteousness, holiness and of fire.

In Jesus Christ name I pray, Amen.

If you prayed this prayer and really meant it, I Believe you have received the miracle of salvation

Prayerfully seek a Bible believing, Holy Spirit filled Church and become a member there.

Ask them to baptize you and teach you the ways of Christ.

Or contact us if you need guideline.

The Unfamiliar Touch
(Lessons from the woman with the issue of Blood)

About the Author

Bishop Dr. Joseph C. Kanu has a medical background but was called by God to serve Him drastically through several visions, dreams, Prophecies and Confirmations.

He resisted God's calling for as long as he could but had to surrender to God's will in 2012 in London United Kingdom when God allowed every other door in his life to become shut but left the door to God's house open to him.

He attended Bible School in London United Kingdom. He has an honorary doctorate for his accomplishments in God's kingdom. He also holds the title: Defender of the faith and other titles. He was set apart as a Bishop Elect

The Unfamiliar Touch
(Lessons from the woman with the issue of Blood)

and later consecrated into the office of a Bishop by the College of Bishops in London United Kingdom.

He is a Song Writer, Singer and Worshipper. He has written and produced his own songs and albums such as: Reggae Praise Medley, Redemption blood, Worship Medley Experience, The Man of Galilee, Praise Experience Medley, Your name is Rapha and Don't give up on Jesus (Rap Song).

He is also an intercessor and has produced
My prayer and prophecies for you (Audio).

He has also written several other books. Such as:

- Making room for your miracles.
  (Lessons from the Shunamite)

The Unfamiliar Touch
(Lessons from the woman with the issue of Blood)

- How to hear from God everyday

- The Unfamiliar Touch (Lesson from the woman with the issue of blood) to mention but a few.

- Living everyday under open heavens
  (lessons from Jacob's life)

- The Ministerial offices (Ethics and Etiquettes)

- Prayers That Availeth much

- Passover and Pentecost
(Their Power and Purpose)

The Unfamiliar Touch
(Lessons from the woman with the issue of Blood)

He was ordained as an Evangelist in London and later on as a Pastor In Assemblies of God Church. He has served and trained as a minister in different churches such as RCCG, AG, BLW CFAN to mention but a few.

He was personally trained and imparted by the Late Evangelist Reinhard Bonke and his team when he was a student of his school of Evangelism in London.

He also received impartation and teaching from Benny Hinn, and late Morris Cerrulo to mention but a few

He runs School of Supernatural Ministry in London where he teaches and equips ministers to move in the Supernatural. He is the presiding Bishop of Rapha Christian Centre house of Healing London and also the President of Bishop Joseph Global Ministries.

The Unfamiliar Touch
(Lessons from the woman with the issue of Blood)

He travels the world with the message of God's kingdom, demonstrating the power of God in the Prophetic, Healing, Miraculous and Deliverance Ministries.

He is married to a British Citizen from South America/ Carribean Island Of Barbados and they are blessed with children.

The Unfamiliar Touch
(Lessons from the woman with the issue of Blood)

Contact Details

Bishop Dr. Joseph C. Kanu

Presiding Bishop Rapha Christian Centre house of Healing London

And President of Bishop Joseph Global Ministries

36 Pitlake Croydon

London United Kingdom

Cr0 3RA

+4478 31 62 52 42

Email: Bishopjosephkanu@gmail.com

www.ingramcontent.com/pod-product-compliance
Lightning Source LLC
Chambersburg PA
CBHW022358040426
42450CB00005B/244